LOVE & MARRIAGE

A Survival Guide

Francis H. Wise, Ph.D.

Second Edition

WISE PUBLISHING COMPANY
wiselearntoread.com
WOODLAND HILLS, CALIFORNIA

LOVE & MARRIAGE

A Survival Guide

Francis H. Wise, Ph.D.

Second Edition

Editor: J. M. Wise

Copyright © 2017
wiselearntoread.com
ISBN: 978-0-915766-83-3

Preface

Love & Marriage, A Survival Guide is an updated version of *Love Affairs*, published by Dr. Wise in 1986. This version of *Love & Marriage* reveals to couples the pitfalls of sexual behavior and guides them on how to sustain a loving, respectful romance in marriage. Marriage is not for everyone. Judge for yourself if marriage is for you. Read what leads to an affair and how fragile love affairs really are.

In order to feel secure and happy, both man and woman must gain enough skills and knowledge for living together and maintaining a household. Learning how to keep love alive will help the couple find unity in their marriage. Couples need to take pride in their home. A home is a place to be at peace with one another.

One chapter reveals how rearing of children affects a marriage. Clues are given on how to protect the sanctity of the marriage vows.

Learn how love affairs are hurtful to couples because of ignorance and fear. Fear comes from the silent thoughts of our mind which society doesn't talk about. These are the things written here that were never taught. As your knowledge increases on how to maintain love and how to defend marriage against the destructive forces in today's society, you will become more secure, less fearful and have a better chance for a happier marriage.

Finally, find out what four international wars have done to our heterosexual relationships. Know that sex is not always satisfying and why. There are many more questions answered about love and marriage.

Authors

Francis H. Wise, psychologist, practiced in Los Angeles, Sherman Oaks, and Thousand Oaks, California, for many years as a psychotherapist. He counseled many parents, (married and divorced), children of all ages, couples and businessmen and women with various personal and family problems over the years.

Dr. Wise has degrees in education, religion, sociology, psychology, and social studies. He attended Willamette University, Oregon College of Education, Oregon State, University of Oregon, Harvard University, Burton University, Union Theological Seminary, Oberlin Theological Seminary, the University of the Philippines in Manila, University of Southern California, University of California Los Angeles and University of Illinois.

Dr. Wise taught Sunday school classes since he was a teenager in Oregon. After graduating from the University of Oregon, he received his masters degree at USC, and from Burton University a doctor's degree in psychology. He worked in the three largest churches in Los Angeles leading all kinds of youth activities. He was a chaplain in the United States Air Force for seven years and spent thousands of hours counseling hospital patients and those in the stockade. He was with the Armed Forces in Japan, Korea, Vietnam, and the Philippines where he received a second doctorate in Psychology.

Dr. Wise taught grade school, high school, and college classes, holding credentials as an elementary and high school teacher in both California and Oregon.

For the Boy Scouts of America, Dr. Wise was a cub master, scoutmaster, explorer and advisor. He wrote and produced a radio show for a year in Texas, and spent four summers as a craft instructor as well as an assistant camp director for the boys camp in Vermont, a Y.M.C.A. Camp in Virginia and at Camp Allegheny in West Virginia.

Dr. Wise authored *Youth & Drugs*, printed by Associated Press, 1973. He also authored a beginning reader series for children, entitled *Dr. Wise Learn to Read Series*, and an *Arithmetic Series for beginners*.

Joyce Wise majored in book publishing at UC Northridge. She designed and published with her husband the famous *Learn to Read Series* and *Arithmetic Series For Beginners*. Joyce then authored two storybooks for second graders, *Musette Finds A Friend* and *Musette & Pierre's Family*, along with two beginning grammar books, *Ann's Rebels* and *Ann Goes To School*. She has rewritten and updated this new version of *Love & Marriage, A Survival Guide*, her husband's life's work for all to enjoy.

Franklin Wise has redesigned and engineered *Love & Marriage, A Survival Guide* to reflect today's attitudes. He has a Bachelor of Science in psychology from the University of Santa Barbara and is also a successful programming engineer.

Acknowledgments

Thank you Katalin Joo, my Desktop Publishing teacher, who patiently taught me Illustrator and InDesign. It was her thorough knowledge and skill as a teacher that made this publication possible. When I wanted to quit, she gave me the courage to fight through the difficult tasks of perfecting my skill towards a more professional look. Thank you Kata.

Thank you to Karen Robbins, my art and Photoshop teacher, who brought me into the world of designing art. Without her confidence in me and her expertise in design, I would not have succeeded. Yes, Karen, I was listening when you lectured.

Note

All names used throughout this book are fictitious and any resemblances to persons living or dead are purely coincidental.

The universal 'he' is used instead of 'he' and 'she,' in order to avoid awkwardness for the reader.

TABLE OF CONTENTS

Part IV - The Future Of Love & Marriage

Gratitude is the spice of life.
It is the pleasant glow of the candle of love
that dispels greed, hate, self-serving, and loneliness.

Part I - Dating

CHAPTER 1

IS MARRIED LOVE FOR EVERYONE?

Loving another person is one of the most fantastic, exhilarating, sky-rocketing experiences of one's lifetime. Unfortunately, for millions of couples, this kind of love does not continue forever. As a psychologist in private practice, Dr. Wise has heard the disappointments of failed love relationships between husbands and wives and parents and child. This is why everyone should know more about love and marriage.

For over fifty percent of the couples who marry, this wonderful experience of loving another individual will end in divorce.[1] These couples have proven, at least for the first time around, that married love may not be successful for everyone. The divorce rate has caused thousands of unwed individuals to fear married love. If everyone knew more about the realities of married love, there would be less fear and a lower divorce rate.

In comparison to marriage, dating love is carefree. It's a time for fun and a time to please each other. It's a time of high emotions; a time for all kinds of feelings, particularly physical—kissing, hugging, back rubbing and sexual sat-

---

[1] Bureau of Census no longer provides one percentage for the number of divorces in the U.S. as it has become very complicated to get an exact figure. First marriages before 1969 lasted longer than marriages after that date when the new law changed to 'no-fault divorce,' making it easy to get a divorce.

isfaction. It is not usually a time for serious commitments. Teenagers and adults eagerly seek dating love. With this kind of excitement it is easy to say, "I love you."

Why do many dating individuals lack the qualifications for married love?

For millions of individuals, the fear of love and the inability to make love last begins the day they are born, especially if they experience quarrelsome, devastating relationships with their parents. Listening to argumentative parents does not teach a child how to resolve disagreeable experiences in a loving manner. It is these unhappy experiences with parents and siblings that cause the fear and the inability to love another person. When these children enter school, they may have difficulties relating to other children. Instead of learning how to get along affectionately, they may become worse. The unaffectionate relationships and the underdeveloped social skills of some children with whom they play may also make them fearful and unfit for marriage.

Every child, at one time or another, has been called names, shoved or pushed and/or overlooked for a deserved recognition. Some have not been picked for a team at school, or been invited to a birthday party or have not gotten something they wanted. Others have had birthdays forgotten, and on and on with the disappointments.

Too many pains, fears and hurts in love relationships during childhood can cause an individual as a teenager or an adult to feel anger, bitterness, jealousy, insecurity and sometime revenge toward a parent, lover, spouse, or an ex-spouse, sibling, or friend. In time, as the abused teenager matures, many bad feelings may be forgotten. But some times, however, they continue, creating apprehensive feelings about love and marriage and failing to make friendships and love succeed. Unfortunately, many of these adults maintain destructive or rejected feelings of their adolescent years for a lifetime. Their love remains immature. These are the individuals that many times never get beyond the dating game and never marry.

There are other individuals who do not have these painful relationships with others and have a healthy relationship with family and friends, but they choose not to marry for one reason or another. Perhaps marriage is not necessarily for everyone.

The purpose of dating is to find out if a couple should marry. Many times a person is in love with love and cannot see beyond the romantic side of dating. A lover may completely miss the warning signs of an immature lover or lover with addictions or personality difficulties. It is for this reason that couples need to seek counseling before marriage or take pre-marital courses to discover if they are suited for each other. Hopefully, the couple will begin to see their partner in a more realistic light.

Dealing with destructive behavior

Dating couples need training on how to recognize destructive attitudes of their partner that will eventually destroy their love if not resolved. If they are to succeed in marriage, the following four destructive characteristics need to be addressed and hopefully corrected while still dating:

3

1. Addressing fears, past hurts, and maladjusted behavioral patterns due to being a child and a teenager;

2. Overcoming the lack of parental training;

3. Correcting mistakes — one's own or another person's with love, without belittling and

4. Dealing harmoniously with serious conflicts.

Correcting these conditions is what therapists are trained to do.

Training couples in human relationships and maintenance of a household go hand and hand.

To have a joyful marriage, a couple must gain a lot of knowledge about human relationships. There is a need to understand yourself and others, particularly one's spouse. There must be shared leisure-time activities. **Excellent manners are a must.**

If a husband had a parent who trained him in manners, and he marries a similarly trained lover, the couple can have a happy marriage. For marriages that are successful, these couples have had the qualifications for success either before marriage or acquired them after marriage.

If a new wife has had no training in sharing household responsibilities before marriage and has not learned the importance of being a homemaker or sharing activities with family members, being social or personal, she will have a difficult time adjusting to married life. But on the other hand, if she has had some training in sharing with family members and maintenance of a household, she will likely adjust far better than if she has had no training at all.

Why do some daters live with each other?

There are many reasons why couples decide to live together instead of marrying. Many times it is for financial reasons — deciding two can live as cheaply as one. Since many couples know little about each other, they decide that sharing expenses would be a good way to see if they are compatible.

Other couples have a definite fear of marriage because of past experiences with family and/or hearing terrible stories from friends about divorce. Many of these couples find that they are not suitable for each other and separate within a year. Some couples live together for five or more years and then separate discovering they can't stand each other. Some do have children and marry and do succeed in having a good life together.

Time will tell if the trend of living together will increase or decrease as time passes.

Does one always need to go to a therapist?

No. If a person is willing to change and his or her partner is mature, their relationship can continue.

It is important for dating couples to find out if there are serious problems of addiction to alcohol, drugs or other diseases that may cause a divorce if they marry. If this is the case, the couple definitely needs a therapist's help if they intend to marry.

If anyone is afraid of marrying for the first or second time, it is not difficult to find out if the fear of failure is justified. An appointment with a psychologist to be tested for marital success will determine whether some or extensive psychotherapy is needed or whether the fear of failure is groundless.

What are the psychosomatic pains that will respond to psychotherapy?

The severe illnesses of love can cause back pains, headaches, sleepless nights, depressions, overwhelming fears, nausea, lack of self-confidence or even anger. The helplessness of an unsolvable situation can cause one to cry uncontrollably, to scream, to hit, to destroy property, or to have suicidal thoughts. These outbursts are a cry for help.

Why is dating love not enough?

By dividing divorced individuals into four groups, it will be easier to understand why dating love is not enough to succeed in marriage and why married love fails.

1. The impossible group: Thousands of homosexuals and bisexuals try a heterosexual marriage.

2. The high risk group: These individuals can be alcoholic, psychotic, drug addicted, wife beaters, child abusers, certain types of neurotics or criminals.

3. The sexually maladjusted group: They cannot engage in wholesome, normal sex. They are pre-mature, frigid, insatiable, promiscuous, frustrated, etc.

4. The teen group: Those who marry before eighteen are in the high risk group.

Today the world is changing so fast, we can hardly keep up with all the new advances in science and technology. These four divorce groups also have been changing. For one, the homosexual community had petitioned the courts in our nation to redefine marriage to include homosexual marriages legal. In 2015, the Supreme Court declared gay marriages to be legal nationwide, however, in some state counties this issue is still under debate. Did God make a mistake? No. He doesn't make mistakes. So why the difficulty with the sexes? We now do not have the answers, but in time they will be revealed to us. So, in the meantime, homosexuals married to heterosexual partners will drop drastically, positively affecting the divorce rate.

If thirty percent of the divorced group had taken family courses during high school and had psychotherapy, they could have made married love succeed. While these couples were getting divorced, changes in our society were happening so fast with the onset of the Tech Age.

Occurring in the next decade or so, the professional healers (psychologists, psychiatrists and family counselors) are gaining the experience to help clients with addiction and personalty disorders. The scientific community will also increase their knowledge when dealing with brain malfunctions. These professionals will also be the miracle workers in lowering the divorce rate.

Over the years, clubs (such as Alcoholic Anonymous, Al-Anon, Overeater's Anonymous, Gamblers Anonymous, etc.), have been established across the nation to help families and their loved ones with serious addiction and personality problems. These clubs have helped dissolve a lot of anger, resentment, lack of control, fears, etc. that have built up over time. Alcoholism is a disease and is not curable, but can be controlled through abstinence as these clubs have discovered. They have helped thousands of family members cope with their loved ones' addiction. They have also helped thousands of addicted individuals abstain from drinking alcohol.

In many severe cases, the only hope for married love to succeed is to see a professional — psychiatrist, psychologist or marriage counselor.

Why is married love better than dating love?

After weeks, months, or sometimes years, only a few dating couples are satisfied with dating love. While everyone acknowledges that dating love is wonderful, most individuals want to believe that married love is even better, including divorced couples. Many who divorce do marry for a second or third time. These are the individuals who convince most of us that married love is the prize one must have.

CHAPTER 2

THE FRUSTRATIONS OF MALES & FEMALES

Few people will disagree that a man can have sexual intercourse and sexual desire with little thought of love. Some say that man's biological system makes him this way. Being sexually irresponsible and unaffectionate during intercourse is a source of frustration for any wife or woman.

Her demands for affection and attention during sexual intercourse, in turn, frustrate many a man.

Why do so many males sexually frustrate females?

There are a variety of causes:

1. The chief cause may be that most parents totally ignore a boy's masturbation activity. They also fail to realize how damaging this activity can be to adult sexual intercourse.

2. Another cause can be the parents' lack of knowledge on how the male child sexually develops, therefore, they are at a loss on how to teach him sexual control.

3. Still another cause may be associated with the societal norms of masculinity (the masculine code of men), which originate largely from military service. This code causes men to segregate physical pleasure from mental affection.

All these causes can be responsible for a woman feeling affectionately frustrated during intercourse.

Females and males are trained differently

The future stresses and quarrels between husband and wife, parent and child begin with parents anxiously teaching radically different sexual roles to their children based on their sex. Note the contrast in how a daughter and a son are traditionally trained:

The female's training

While boys are being trained this way, girls are taught to be sexually restrained; they can get pregnant. Fathers and mothers teach girls that they can only indulge in sexual intercourse if they love a man and he loves them. To have sexual intercourse in other ways is to be a 'slut' or a 'whore.' Thus, the sexual conflict between man and woman is seeded. As the female is encouraged by her parents and other adults to have loving, caring feelings towards others. She is given dolls, dishes, a doll house with miniature furniture, and pretty clothing. She is gently treated and trained in feminine attitudes characteristic of women, not shared by men. She soon gets the idea that she is to take care of things (housekeeping) as well as family members.

When a girl discovers that she can have babies, she should naturally develop a responsible attitude toward sexual intercourse, as this discovery generates in her affectionate feelings, caring for another person, and the desire to be protective toward the ones she loves. She soon knows that her destiny is to be a mother and a wife when she marries.

The Frustrations Of Males & Females

Some females are taught to be sexually fearful

When a female relates to a male, if her parents are fearful of pregnancy, of a wrong choice for a mate, of promiscuity or of sexual molestation, they tend to over-restrict her activities because they do not trust her or any male to be sexually controlled.

Her parents' fears can severely affect her love relationships, and as a result their daughter may become overly fearful or overly bold as a reaction to her parents' fears. This fear can cause frigidity or other sexual maladjustments. Probably thirty percent or more of the females are frigid. Frigidity is without a doubt the cause of many illicit affairs.

The male's training

Mother tries to teach her son to be a loving, caring individual, but she does not necessarily prepare him to be a father or a husband.

Father's insistence that there be a radical difference in the training of the sexual roles between son and daughter often contributes to the sexual difficulty of his children as adults.

Father thinks that it takes a tough, rough attitude for a male to survive and to protect his family. So Father frustrates the efforts of Mother who tries to teach her son tender, affectionate concern for the family.

Many fathers teach their boys to hit, hurt, and to seek fame, fortune and adventure. A few fathers teach their sons to roam.

Some fathers allow their boys to think and act destructively in their play activities and to exploit others for their own glory and personal gain.

He is taught not to be a "sissy." He is taught thereby to think of himself as superior to women.

He looks at girls as athletically inferior and weak in physical strength. Not only does he have a penis to make him feel superior, but he has big muscles, too. Everyone has heard boys say, "She can't play. She doesn't know how. She's too weak." Even though these statements may not be true, many boys maintain this attitude.

Not only does Father help develop his son's attitude about being a man, but also other men do, too.

Men freely talk of sexual intercourse while boys are in their presence. They talk about how great intercourse is. They have calendars of nude women. They talk about how great it is to lay one. They even tease boys and ask them if they have gotten any yet.

"Don't bother with that love nonsense, Son," Father may say. Boys also hear old sayings like "Love 'em and leave 'em" or "Keep 'em barefooted and pregnant."

Seeing sex on TV and hearing remarks made by older boys and men may even cause a six-year-old boy to think about sexual intercourse as an act of personal, sexual pleasure rather than an act of mutual affection and caring.

Thus, boys begin at an early age thinking about 'laying girls' and not making babies. Boys develop a responsible attitude towards sexual intercourse much later than girls. Some males never learn it.

Destructive masturbation attitudes and feelings

What all parents should probably fear and react to is a boy's masturbation fantasies. His uncontrolled thinking is probably why a male attempts to have intercourse with their daughter. These masturbation fantasies may be, surprisingly, the real source of trouble to a dating couple as well as a married couple.

As if the males' training in being irresponsible and sexually exploiting were not enough to cause marital difficulties, masturbation further develops attitudes and feelings that can make males even more irresponsible and inconsiderate in adult sexual activities with women.

By nine or ten years of age, many boys are masturbating. By the teen years the figures may be as high as ninety percent.

Although little research has been done on this subject, according to many Christian Church leaders, children and adults should not masturbate. The Catholics and the Mormons leaders are particularly against it.

I am not convinced that it is a healthy habit because it encourages boys to have serious misunderstandings about sexual intercourse and affectionate relationships between the sexes — male and female.

CHAPTER 2

The culprit of masturbation

What really intensifies a boy's enjoyment while fantasizing is the imaginary sexual intercourse he has with a girl or woman while stroking his penis. Certainly the physical stroking is not harmful, but fantasizing about women while doing this is harmful. Usually this fantasy is with a girl or woman he knows. This might be an aunt, the woman next door, or some woman he has seen on TV or in a magazine. He might even masturbate while looking at the centerfold of *Playboy*.

Trying to experience the real sexual act and what it feels like through imagination, leads boys into all kinds of peeping and mental undressing of girls and women.

A therapy study

The police referred to me a fourteen-year-old boy client. He had been caught peeping through windows at women while they undressed in their bedrooms. He told me that there are many women who don't pull down their shades.

He had a regular route for frequenting stores that sold periodicals and books to look at sexual magazines. He knew when the new issues were being delivered to the different stores. He also had a route for looking into garbage cans for sexual magazines that were thrown out. Peeping took a lot of his time.

Amazingly, he didn't date girls. His excitement came from masturbating and thinking about the women he had seen undressing and in magazines.

THE FRUSTRATIONS OF MALES & FEMALES

After several hours of therapy he told me that I had ruined his sex life. He no longer enjoyed sexual magazines or peeping into woman's bedrooms. His curiosity had been satisfied, so he didn't need to peep any more.

This is what psychotherapy is about. Talking a person into or out of wrong behavioral patterns. A good therapist gains his client's trust so that he can change or diminish hurtful attitudes. At the same time the therapist's suggestions to his client are constructive. Many times it takes hours of therapy before a client accepts constructive behavioral patterns.

Fantasizing breeds promiscuity

After listening to hundreds of hours of men and boys' masturbation thinking, I have concluded that fantasizing is probably the beginning of adult promiscuity.

Fantasies can also cause maladjustments in married love and sexual intercourse for the following reasons:

1. The intense feeling during ejaculation causes a boy to think that this is the only reason for adult sexual intercourse. In the mind of boys, it creates the idea that the female is only valuable because he can have intercourse with her.

2. In the mind of the masturbator, fantasies justify having illicit sexual affairs. Fantasies do not encourage males to be sexually loyal to a woman, but just the opposite. A male may have imaginary affairs with a hundred women by age twenty without any social disapproval.

CHAPTER 2

3. Imaginary sexual thinking, unchecked by reality, sanctions lustful, erotic, promiscuous thoughts instead of feelings of appreciation, concern, and caring for a female. This thinking may also explain why many males lack affectionate feelings toward the female while engaged in sexual activities.

4. A male's imaginary fantasies may cause him to be premature during intercourse as an adult. This may be because he has not had to control himself while masturbating hundreds of times. He also has never had to consider a woman's feelings and desires, nor has he ever had to deal with sexual timing. These sexual fantasies could arrest a boy's sexual development at the masturbation level for the rest of his life.

5. Ejaculating after a few strokes of intercourse will seriously disturb both the husband and wife emotionally as neither will feel satisfied. Both will feel disappointed.

6. Fantasizing during hundreds of masturbation experiences may make a male sexually selfish and self-centered.

7. Sometimes a woman is an excessive masturbator and fantasizer. In this case, she might not be able to reach a climax or have an orgasm unless she depends upon her fantasies to carry her through the sex act.

The cause of frustration for many woman

A wife can be very disappointed and feel she is being used by her husband and not loved. Her justification for sexual intercourse is to have babies and/or to be loved. But the big physical enjoyment for boys is ejaculation. For many men it will remain this way in that sexual pleasure may be only in the act of ejaculation, not kissing, holding, or physical nearness. Many men are not concerned with their partner's sexual pleasure or in sharing sexual pleasure — be it with their wives or girlfriends. A feeling of being used and not loved can cause the wife to become involved with another man while married.

An illicit affair without intercourse

Masturbation also leads to having illicit sexual affairs without actual sexual intercourse.

One of my female clients told me of one such way. A businessman employed her to come to his office on a regular basis. She took her clothes off and walked nude in front of him while he masturbated. Can you imagine the turn on? When he finished, she put on her clothes and he handed her twenty dollars.

The dream affair

Dreaming during sleep about affairs is another way of having imaginary sexual intercourse for a male and a female. This can be very exciting and almost as good as the real experience. The dream may have been provoked by some sexual event during the day's activity.

When a male dreams about having sexual intercourse, he sees the female kissing him while feeling her nude body and hears her whisper sweet nothings to him. The dream is so real and enjoyable that he ejaculates without touching his penis.

Many boys have thought there was something wrong with them the first two or three times this happened. They were greatly relieved when someone told them that this is called a 'wet dream.' These dreams are harmless and are normal. They happen infrequently.

Women need emotional involvement to feel complete

Unfortunately, most women are not aware of the fantasizing that goes on in boys and men's minds about sex. If they were, as mothers they might train their sons to think differently. They also might not marry men who have become arrested in their sexual development at the masturbation level. Women refer to the ejaculation after only a few strokes of intercourse as the 'rabbit' approach or the other expression they use is "Wham, bang, thank you Ma'am."

There are men who continue to masturbate after marriage which frequently pushes either, or both of them, into an affair.

A woman needs admiration, appreciation, sharing, and being taken care of — not feeling like a servant or parent. She needs also to engage in some form of emotional involvement with the male to feel complete.

When a woman thinks about a love affair with a man, she thinks of an emotional, caring relationship, not just sexual intercourse. When a married or single man talks to a woman about love, he may be acting out his masturbation fantasies. His relationships with both his wife and his mistress may be only sexual. He may be irresponsible sexually and really uncaring due to his masturbation habits.

Effects of masturbation

Men have told me that while having sexual intercourse with their wives, they think of another women. This frequently is the only way they can continue to have sexual activities with their wives. This is another imaginary version of having an affair.

Women have also told me that while having intercourse with their husbands, they frequently have fantasies about other men. Sometimes they tell themselves sexual jokes to get turned on if their husbands are not affectionate.

The husband who ejaculates too quickly causes the wife not to reach an orgasm. To achieve an orgasm she may masturbate herself. These actions on the part of the wife may be caused by the male's masturbation attitudes.

Is it real love if a spouse thinks about another when making love?

Could this be mutual masturbation without either of them knowing it? It may be the fantasy of promiscuity, not love that produces sexual satisfaction. Many times it is the fantasy that continues the marriage relationship.

Will this kind of sexual intercourse unite a couple or cause one of them to seek an affair or a divorce? Without

19

emotional involvement, without knowing why the sexual act feels empty or frustrated, there is much disappointment in this type of marriage

Sexual knowledge of masturbation fantasies and sexual training should cause every male to examine his sexual thinking, his sexual conversations and his love motivations.

Isn't this the kind of love information everyone ought to know?

Without it, how does a man or a woman know whether he or she is experiencing real love?

Chapter 3

Is Sex Always Satisfying?

As a teenager, I have always heard men say that sexual intercourse with a woman was the most exciting experience on earth. Therefore, I thought most men had satisfying sexual experiences. As a therapist, I had to correct my youthful misconceptions. Year after year, I sit and hear all the difficulties couples have with sexual intercourse. Sometimes I wonder why they bother to become sexually involved. Clients have said that sexual intercourse is a disturbing, frustrating, not at all satisfying experience. Some male clients tell me, "I can't get an erection." Others say, "When I insert it, it goes limp." Still others say, "After fifty strokes, I ejaculate. Am I disappointed!" Needless to say, the difficulties and disappointments are many. Let's explore why some sexual activities are disturbing especially when they are erotically motivated.

When is sex considered erotic?

If you are a Christian, then erotic is any sexual activity that is forbidden by the church. Psychologically, sexual activities are erotic when a person engages in them for selfish pleasure only and not for the pleasure of the other person. Sometimes the only pleasure of an erotic act is the fact that it is forbidden.

Observe how women change their fashion styles yearly. For some women these changes add spice to life.

Many times, however, women engage in extreme fashions because they are forbidden by parents, clergymen and politicians —usually for sexual reasons. This extreme is called sexual advertising for the female. These women advertise their bodies to gain the attention of men; others do it to gain freedom from sexual moral condemnation. An erotic act is frequently a defiant act or an act to satisfy curiosity. The person performing the erotic act usually has no moral concern. Sometimes it is an insatiable act, as in the case of the nymphomaniac. The thrill for the transvestite is in wearing clothes of the opposite sex, because it is forbidden.

For some individuals, the only satisfying sexual experience they have are considered abnormally erotic by others. They can now belong to erotic clubs which hold conventions.

Here are some abnormally forbidden erotic acts:

1. Unless the husband ties his wife up, he is not interested. If she doesn't tie him up and beat him, why have sex?

2. Some men and women must draw blood or cause mental anguish before they can perform.

3. Some men want a different woman for every day of the year.

4. Some men and women only want group sex.

5. Some men like to swap wives.

6. Some men only like prostitutes.

7. Some men are not content until they get married,

have a steady mistress and then enjoy both women. Sometimes they line the mistress up a month or so before the wedding.

8. Some men have fetishes. The wife must wear certain kinds of clothing or shoes for them to get excited, or vice versa.

9. Some men can only perform if a woman wears a certain kind of perfume.

10. Some men and women find animals more satisfying than human beings. They really are more interested in dogs, sheep, or deer. Years ago in Griffith Park at the Los Angeles Zoo, officials caught a man coming over the fence to have sexual intercourse with a deer.

11. Some men can only have intercourse with a woman after oral sex.

12. Some men are into anal sex with their wives. That's all they want.

13. Some men and women can only perform after a quarrel.

14. Some men and women must use profanity during intercourse.

15. Some men have to imagine having sex with another woman while stroking their wife.

16. Some men and women only want to do it with children.

17.   Some men only want a woman to masturbate them, none of that putting a penis into a woman for
them.

18.   Some want sexual activities with both men and
women — the bisexuals. A guy may look better than a dame,
or vice versa.

19.   Some men want sexual activities only with other
men — the homosexuals have more difficulties having satisfying sexual relationships than the heterosexuals, as they are
only into erotic sexual activities.

20.   Some men and women are celibates who do not
want to have sexual intercourse with anyone. There are all
kinds of reasons for being a celibate. I thought, as a teenager,
there was only one reason — religion. Wrong!

Are sexual deviations satisfying?

For men and women who practice sexual deviations,
wholesome lovemaking is not only a bore, but it is also ab-
solutely impossible. They can only get sexual satisfaction
through sexual deviations. These people are at odds with
themselves. Clients, who practice deviations, tell me that
sexual deviations are exciting, but unsatisfying sexual activities. Why?

1. There is a fear of being caught by the police.
2. There is moral disapproval.
3. There is danger in approaching the wrong person.
4. There is a lack of fulfillment.

IS SEX ALWAYS SATISFYING?

Do women enjoy erotic activities?

Most women do not enjoy these erotic activities with their husbands and can become very emotionally distressed. Their moral conscience is being violated. If their husbands are physically abusive and possessive, they feel trapped. There seems to be no physical escape. Whatever escapes they use depend upon the kind of husband they have. Some are driven to masturbation, to affairs, to divorce and a few to suicide or celibacy.

Some women have the same erotic sexual range as men:

1. Some only want oral sex. Keep that penis out.
2. Some only want anal sex.
3. Some like intercourse with three guys during the week or all three at once. Others like to tie men up and whip them.
4. Some even like dogs.
5. Some women use vibrators, dildos, pillows, cucumbers, etc.
6. Some teenage girls are into sexual fads. One of my teenage girl clients told me what the rage was one summer. The girls wanted to feel what it was like to get pregnant. They got pregnant and sixty days later had abortions. Another fad for the summer was that some girls wanted to feel what it was like to get pregnant by the same boy. Then the two of them could compare sexual notes, and then get abortions. Another teenage girl client discovered that her girl friend was a virgin. So she persuaded her boyfriend to have intercourse with her while she watched and gave instructions.

7. Then there are lesbians who prefer females. One of them will usually play the role of a male. They will usually act out the heterosexual patterns of behavior.

As with men, I can write pages on the different ways in which women prefer erotic activities. After listening to a variety of sexual practices of men and women, one wonders what is normal sexual intercourse.

To anyone considering marriage, it should be a little unnerving to hear or read about all of these erotic sexual acts. Fortunately, most individuals don't know what most professionals hear day in and day out.

Unfortunately, many clients tell me they didn't discover that their spouses were into erotic sexual practices until after they were married. Sometimes a spouse hides it for a year or two before exposing him or herself. Usually men wait until women are pregnant to reveal their erotic behavior patterns. The women then are trapped into the relationship, or vice versa.

Is there wholesome sex out there?

Yes. There is wholesome sexual intercourse. It is exclusive — only with a spouse and no one else. There is no masturbation, no affair with another person, and no telling yourself sexual stories to maintain sexual activities with your spouse.

It is an exclusive sexual relationship.

It is caring about the lover's various kinds of sexual and emotional feelings.

Is Sex Always Satisfying?

It is the willing acceptance of being responsible for the care of another person — husband, wife, or child.

It is the joyful sharing of feelings, ideas, activities, moneys, and material things.

It is going to bed with admiration, appreciation of what one's spouse has been doing for you all day.

It is an awareness on the man's part that a woman has been taught that sexual intercourse is only possible when a man cares for her. For her to have intercourse on any other basis is to prostitute oneself.

Wholesome sexual intercourse does not cause a woman to think that she is a prostitute. She needs to know that her affection, her talents, her physical caring for the family members, her sense of humor, her character, her fun ways of living are just as important to her husband as her sex organ, or his ejaculation.

He knows that he is more important than the salary he brings home. He knows that she appreciates him for his character, his affection, his being a parent to their children. He is more important than his status. She didn't marry him to escape living with her father and mother.

When in bed, as the couple hug and kiss, they not only have sexual desires for each other, but they also desire to consummate love feelings through sexual intercourse. They can't get enough of each other in the time they spend together or through their shared activities. They look forward to sleeping with each other night after night. Sexual intercourse is an activity they can share each day. They do not limit their sexual activities to once or twice a week.

Since their life together is exciting and interesting, there is little time to be bored. How then can sexual activities be boring?

Everyone should know that unsatisfying sexual experiences can cause a loss of affection and appreciation and respect for one another.

Part II - Marriage

Chapter 4

Courtesy Sustains Love

Courtesy is an attitude, a basic acknowledgment that **no one owes you anything**. It is the emotional feeling of love. It is translated into workable, sensible relationships. It is the discipline that sustains the love feeling into a lasting relationship, whether between husband and wife, parent and child, or friends. It strengthens affection and appreciation between husband and wife.

Courtesy is an attitude that creates appreciation. This basic acknowledgment is the basis of a continuing love relationship between husband and wife, child and parent, brother and sister.

Without courtesy love withers, children become unruly and family life becomes unhappy. Illicit affairs can then happen.

Why isn't courtesy appreciated and practiced more?

Courtesy is more than detailed procedures for important social occasions. The spirit of affectionate concern for another person's rights and privileges seems to get lost when reading about etiquette in a book, such as in *Rules & Rituals For Social Occasions*. These rules and rituals detail the procedures for weddings and formal occasions, but tend to obscure the affectionate concerns of the individual.

You say 'please' because you recognize that the other person isn't required to do what you ask. You are imposing upon that person's positive attitude, good-will and generosity. That person may be morally obligated to do what you request. It may be the sensible way to relate to you, but he or she doesn't have to do what you want. You also say 'thank you' to the person for the same reason, even though you pay him or her a salary or a fee to do what is requested. He or she doesn't really have to do it.

Professionals, from mechanics to doctors to lawyers, can tell a person to take their money and go away if a client has an abusive or unappreciative attitude.

Respect is the keystone of love.

No one falls in love with a person that he or she cannot respect. When a husband or wife loses respect for each other, either an affair or divorce will occur, or they will have an enduring quarrelsome relationship. When children lose respect for their parents, they become troublemakers.

Courtesy details how one should render respect to a person, a group or an object. The word "respect" means that a person thinks someone or something is worthwhile. Books written on courtesy, politeness, well-mannered and well-bred individuals are called books of etiquette.

Amy Vanderbilt's *Complete Book of Etiquette* successfully organizes social occasions by detailing how to be respectful, to be fair, to be considerate, and to express affection at formal dinners, balls, banquets, weddings, infant baptisms, public receptions, and so on. They detail the formal ways of paying one's respect with courteous behavior.

COURTESY SUSTAINS LOVE

Etiquette books also detail how to entertain infor-
mally. They are guides on how to entertain guests with courtesy at home or in public. But there is no etiquette book that
details how to get along personally, day after day, in a home
with children, parents and spouses. **A daily family etiquette
system is most severely needed for family happiness. There
is also no system for sexual etiquette.**

Why are married love failures so high?

Could a lack of a family etiquette system be the reason? In Europe, centuries ago, parents enrolled sons and
daughters (thirteen to fifteen years of age) in schools of etiquette. Courtesy was considered by the monarchs more important than reading and writing. Only when the printing
press was invented did reading, writing and mathematics
became equally important.

Why didn't public educators continue to teach etiquette?

Probably because public educators didn't think courtesy was that important. Neither did the Protestant clergy or
the parents consider it that important. It still is not important today. The Protestant seminaries of the United States still
do not consider or teach that etiquette is important.

Church leaders do not apparently comprehend that
it is etiquette that disciplines love for a neighbor, nor do they
comprehend that etiquette is essential for the maintenance
of love in a family.

The etiquette system of the colonists was based on
the English system of class distinctions. This system of eti-

quette taught that authority came from the King to his subjects. In keeping with that authority system, children were taught to say, "Yes, sir!" and "Yes, ma'am!" Individuals who had titles insisted on being addressed by them. The system was not addressed to the respect and dignity of the individual, but mainly to the respect of the rank or social position.

George Washington, the first president, set new standards of etiquette for the head of state which reflected that authority came from the governed.

The political leaders of the late 1700s and the 1800s (Washington, Adams, Jefferson, Franklin, and Lincoln), were creating a social system based upon the equality of the individual.

Obviously, educators couldn't support or teach a system of etiquette that paid homage to the King and to a class system after the signing of the Declaration of Independence. Educators today are still teaching the opposite of the King's rule and class structure. They maintain that authority comes from the citizens and that all citizens are equal. So they don't teach the etiquette system of the Crown.

Since there was no national system of etiquette for a democracy, the educators didn't know what to teach. They then left the etiquette system to be taught by parents.

What Happened to the Etiquette System?

The parents taught their children the etiquette system of their geographical regions.

In Virginia, and in many southern states, although modified, the etiquette system of the English Crown was maintained.

In the New England States, it was abandoned. There, the churches, which had originated from the Mayflower, were congregational in government and rejected anything that expressed Church of England worship or class standards. They also rejected a class system because they believed that all men were equal.

The members of the frontier churches of Illinois, Ohio, Iowa, etc. were anti-formal in dress, speech, and behavior. The church services were also informal.

The farther west people traveled from the original thirteen states to live, the less regard they had for formal etiquette.

The school system of the United States today is keeping with the tradition of not teaching etiquette, but only stresses the 3 R's, reading, writing and arithmetic, which refers to the foundation of a basic skills education.

Effects of no etiquette being taught to children

Is leaving the 'E' for etiquette out of the school environment why children are unfair and why they swear and shove?

The public educators of today are still not teaching etiquette, but are teaching the biology of sexual intercourse in the classroom. This instruction unintentionally teaches millions of high school students inconsiderate sexual activity and a mechanistic sexual approach. This kind of teaching of sexual biology stimulates irresponsible and unaffectionate love. Bedroom etiquette or the morality that accompanies it is completely ignored.

The public educators may have no other alternative than to teach an inconsiderate mechanistic sexual approach, thanks to the internal conflict amongst Protestants and between the Protestants and Roman Catholics. The educators have been forced to choose a position of least conflict.

Since leaders of the church, educators and etiquette authors have put the bedroom off limits, there are no agreed upon standards for the bedroom. No wonder so many women are frightened by the bedroom scene. No wonder rape is part of marital sex. Remember, there is still a strong military as well as a macho influence in the bedroom.

The assumption on the part of some males (wife or not) is that a woman is a prostitute. If he pays the room and board, bills, and other expenses, she, by God, better lay down and put out whenever he wants sexual intercourse.

This lack of a sexual etiquette is disturbingly and disappointingly experienced by some divorced women who have been invited out by a man for the first time to dinner. Shortly after they order, the man asks, "Will you or will you not?"

"What?" she asks.

His response, "Have sex with me tonight."

She replies "No, this is a first date."

Courtesy Sustains Love

To her surprise, the date gets up from the table and leaves the restaurant. Such a man is a sexual hunter.

Some men are like hunters, they stalk the prey. There is no sexual courtesy — only a token kind of courtesy. There is little respect for human dignity of a woman or her rights with this approach. They grab what they want and leave a trail of humiliated women.

Some men are rapists. They have been humiliated and have lost many rights and much human dignity. The only way they can solve a basic human sexual need is through a violent sexual relationship and this is more about power and control than it is about sex. They fall into the worst traditions of the sexual hunter. They cannot have a voluntary love affair. They certainly have not been taught etiquette of any kind.

Because sexual etiquette does not exist, many wives get the 'rabbit approach' of the masturbator. He hops on top of his wife and with a few strokes he is finished. He rolls over and is sound asleep. This is not only a lustful approach, but it is an inconsiderate one which could have been avoided by the knowledge of sexual etiquette.

There should be a mutually agreed upon sexual approach that both sexes can enjoy. Until an etiquette system is created, the mistress will frequently get better treatment than the wife.

The opposite effects

However, on the opposite side of the coin, some men are shy and afraid of the sexual encounter. They have no sexual etiquette to guide them either.

Chapter 4

I remember a classmate of mine at Oberlin, telling me how difficult it was for her husband to have sexual intercourse on their wedding night. He could not undress in front of her. She then had to coax him into bed.

It is permissible to have sexual intercourse. The church has blessed the relationship. The state has issued a license permitting it.

Why can't a husband and wife openly communicate their affection and sexual desires to one another?

Why can't they kiss, pet and hug each other's bodies to communicate their love for each other?

Unfortunately, Jesus was very silent and had nothing to say about the sexual etiquette of a husband and wife. Paul had much to say about not having sexual intercourse, but nothing to say about sexual etiquette. Jewish tradition certainly is not silent on this point.

For centuries, most families lived in one bedroom. This may have a lot to do with the lack of sexual etiquette in the bedroom. It may also have a lot to do with silent sexual intercourse. A spouse could easily awaken four to ten children.

The fact that men worked ten hours a day and women gave birth to as many as fifteen children may also have had a lot to do with the lack of sexual etiquette and a lack of etiquette in general.

No wonder the paid mistress seems so exciting. There is an etiquette for playing around. Settings are contrived.

The woman is sought after. There is competition. He is paying a high price for flirting this way. Both take time to be entertaining. Everything is always ready. Dating a mistress has high priority over a man's other activities.

Dating a wife obviously has a low priority for many husbands after five to ten years of marriage. She has now become the household servant. She neglects keeping up the settings for the stage that will keep her marriage interesting. Marriage now becomes a drag and 'old hat' for both of them.

How does a married couple maintain a dating attitude?

One of the obstacles of dating love etiquette can be children. They can and do interfere with a loving relationship between husband and wife.

A colicky baby ends any affectionate relationships for the night. A drug addicted teenager can end a marital relationship entirely.

Children should be taught family etiquette so that they don't interfere with the affectionate relationships of their parents. Parents do need privacy for talking and love making.

Avenues to privacy:

1. Master bedroom doors do need locks.

2. If the bedroom door is closed and father is in the room with mother, children should knock and ask permission to enter. Father may be loving mother.

3. Children should learn that when mother and father go into the bedroom for an hour, the children are not to interrupt them.

4. Once in a while, just for two or three hours, parents should send children out to a baby sitter. Then they can relax and have loving sexual intimacy with each other.

5. Children can eat early. Mother and father can then go to the bedroom as soon as he comes home, snack, talk, and have intimate relations with one another in a relaxed fashion. In this way, their relationship is strengthened. Parents can join the kids later.

6. Children should not sleep in bed with parents. There are many parents who permit this as a regular activity. This certainly interferes with any intimate activities of the parents and teaches the children to be inconsiderate. Only occasionally is sleeping in bed together a good activity for all concerned.

The family should revolve around the affection of mother and father. If the family affection revolves around the children's demands and attention getting methods, this violates the fundamentals of etiquette.

Many children flee from their homes when they become teenagers, as they do not see or feel a loving relationship between their parents due, in part, to a lack of sexual and family etiquette. They no longer consider their parents the entertainers they did before age nine. Little wonder that they cannot express love as adults when they marry.

At 8 p.m. children should be a low priority. Many of them dominate the family scene until 10 p.m., which restricts parents the opportunity for lovemaking or for sharing the day's problems or activities. There is no time to quietly renew or reflect on the events of the day. There should be an etiquette system, not only for the day, but particularly for evening meetings with the family.

These are some of the ways for parents to prevent children from destroying the dating love.

The relationship between husband and wife?

Before marriage, the wife had high priority. Then, she had plenty of excitement. Some wives report that the cat or dog gets more affection because the husband pets the animals while watching TV. Wives can become very jealous of these pets. Many teenage girls are not considering marriage when they see mother treated in this unromantic way. The time has come for, not only a bedroom etiquette, but also a married love etiquette for husbands and wives.

Divorce has increased so rapidly since 1950 that there is no commonly accepted etiquette for anyone to know how to treat children, former spouses, relatives, and also dates. There certainly is a need of an etiquette system for divorced individuals who are dating for the second or third time around.

Who will create a courtesy system?

If the educators and the church leaders are not going to create a courtesy system, who will?

CHAPTER 4

Courtesy, particularly in the bedroom will **help prevent affairs and enrich married love.**

Are these not the thoughts about etiquette that everyone should consider?

CHAPTER 5

WHAT IS THE BEDROOM FOR?

For hundreds and thousands of couples, the bedroom is necessarily a place to sleep with only a closet, a bed and a chest — plain and simple.

A bedroom is not that important to a husband. Probably because, as a child and teenager, he was never allowed to play in his parent's bedroom, as it was off limits to him. He was accustomed to a very plain room, perhaps with a table and chair, a bed and closet to hang a few clothes. Mainly, though, it was just a place to sleep. Thus, many men have never given the bedroom much thought as they were growing up. He never remembers his father and mother ever having sexual intercourse. He just arrived in this environment somehow, but never by route of sexual intercourse. The stork must have brought him. Dad was never in the bedroom. He was in the garage, the backyard, in front of the TV. Only when he was seriously ill did one catch him in bed.

So the U.S. male has probably never learned to live in the bedroom. He doesn't think of sex in the bedroom. He thinks of it in a car, a motel, on the grass or in a sleeping bag— any place but a bedroom at home. He doesn't think of it as a place of entertainment or as a place to talk.

The female, on the other hand, was allowed to go into her parents room to play grown up with mother's high heeled shoes and to watch mother dress, do her hair, and apply makeup. She grew up admiring her mother. She grew up playing dolls and helping mother wash and clean the house.

She has her own ideas about how a bedroom should be and what she would like her bedroom to be when married. Her answer to 'What is a bedroom for?' more than her husband's answer, determines whether the couple will have an affair, a divorce, or a long, happy marriage.

Should the bedroom be exciting or dull?

The bed may be so short in length that only a 5'-3" female can sleep in it comfortably. For a male 6' or taller, it is most uncomfortable. If a tall woman or male wants to spread out, it is impossible. Hundreds of thousands of couples have sexual intercourse in this type of bed for about 10 to 20 minutes, once or twice a week. No couple will spend much more time in this type of bed. Little wonder that, in time, one of the spouses will think about an affair with such little sexual activity going on and in such an unattractive, uncomfortable bedroom.

Thank God, someone invented king and queen sized beds. Men and women spend over 50% of their time sleeping, so if they can afford it, a king or queen sized bed provides a most comfortable physical atmosphere for the couple.

Should it be feminine or masculine?

Should it be frilly or plain, elegant or poverty stricken?

Some women have no consideration for their new husband and decorate the bedroom so feminine that any male would feels out of place in it. There is a closet full of dresses, shoes, and a dresser with all kinds of perfume and make-up on top of it. The decor is delicately feminine. He is afraid to move for fear of breaking something. There is no room for him to fit in — just a feminine atmosphere. For her, the bedroom is a place to store clothes, not a room to share with her husband. She has the big closet filled with clothes. She takes over the husband's closet, the children's closets, and whatever other closets she can. Guess what she wears most of the time — a blouse or sweatshirt with Levis. Her husband soon get the message that her clothes are more important than the rest of the family. Wives who think and act this way about the bedroom can create a divorce.

The wife's vanity may exclude her husband from their affections. This is not a bedroom where a male will feel like reading, watching TV or talking to his wife. In this room a husband is a guest.

What kind of bedroom is conducive for lovemaking?

What kind of bedroom is conducive to sleep, to talk, to be affectionate as well as lovemaking?

For him the bedroom may be strange, intriguing, and erotic. It may be sexually exciting or it may turn him off. But, by and large, the new husband is generally open to whatever his wife desires for both of them. It will depend also upon what he wants and looks for in a woman.

For her the bedroom may be a place to continue the dating relationship. If she has no thought of decor, arrangement, or a plan to keep their love alive, their love will diminish over time.

It will also depend largely upon her background growing up how she will decorate it. Will she reflect both their personalities, or just hers.

It will depend upon how she keeps it, or whether she has no idea how to arrange the room or organize her clothes, his clothes or the incidentals of living.

If she has no idea or has never thought about keeping a bedroom, and doesn't take the responsibility for its arrangement and keep, eventually there is a mess everywhere. Perhaps she is so overwhelmed, hasn't a clue what to do, or doesn't feel it is her job to make the bedroom a special place to keep their love alive. Maybe this is how her parents lived.

A girl who has been trained and prepared for this time in her life knows how to organize her household. As a girl growing up, she dreamed of fixing up her bedroom one day and looked forward to this special occasion. She knows what to do and is responsible for setting up a house to make her family comfortable, especially her and her spouse's bedroom.

What type of bedroom will keep the marriage alive?

For some women it is a place of beauty. It is elegantly decorated to suit both the male and female's taste. It is kept neat and clean. It meets both their needs. They always feel comfortable and warm toward each other in this room.

A bedroom, no doubt, means more to the woman than to the male in the United States. For her, it is romance. A beautiful place to dress. She looks into a full length mirror on the back of a door to admire herself and to be admired. It is a room full of happy memories spent with her husband and her babies. It is a place to be seduced if she can permit this kind of thinking and has that kind of husband. Her husband is a most fortunate man.

What one thinks in the bedroom makes a difference

A bride and groom enter their bedroom for the first time, excited, fearful and full of dreams for the future. The last thought they would ever think of is that the emotional and financial stability does depend upon how they feel and think about each other in the bedroom. Every couple needs to be aware that they need to make the transition in thinking from **dating love** to **married love**.

The newlyweds as they sleep together are just contentedly continuing their dating love experiences, unaware of the future obligations of married love. They are blissfully unaware that their future happiness in the bedroom depends upon their making an easy transition from dating love to married love. Many couples are aware that there is a transition to be made from being single to being married, but what to do about it is a mystery to most of them. So they just hope it will continue to happen.

The **dating couple** has thoughts of admiration, sexual desires, and fun activities to share with each other. They are eager to kiss. Emotionally, she wants him close to her. She has sexual thoughts and so does he. The couple pushes the day's activities out of their minds; thus thinking only of each other. She gets ready for his arrival, and he is in a hurry to get there. Their time together is of the utmost importance. This make the evening exciting, interesting and sexually alive.

By the time the engagement is announced, both may be so preoccupied with thinking and feelings about their love affair that they really don't have time for anything else.

Usually when a woman is dating, what her man does to her physically in bed doesn't matter too much. She is too excited to care. It is his qualities that are attracting her. She has found, she thinks, what she wants. He tells her how important she is to him. This is all she needs to hear. She knows that she has never been this important to anyone.

At least fifty percent of the married couples lose this eagerness, excitement, and illusion of the dating days as the months and years pass.

Why? Because gradually what they are thinking and doing during the day becomes more important than their sexual thinking and affection for each other at night in the bedroom.

Married love may be severely damaged by what a spouse thinks and feels in the bedroom.

At bedtime, if the wife is constantly thinking about P.T.A. meetings or is upset by her husband's lack of attention, or his failure to perform household chores etc., she is not thinking as sexually and affectionately as she did when dating.

At bedtime, if the husband is wondering about his sexual performance, whether it will be acceptable to her, or if he is angry about how she is taking care of the children, or the house, guess what; there is going to be a lack of sexual communication and affection.

She probably has been so busy with activities before going to bed that this has prevented him from kissing and hugging her.

His desire for affection and intercourse has been mounting since late afternoon at work, by nine he is at a point that he can't wait any longer. He probably hasn't told her this. If he has, she has told him, "Later." He has been thinking passionately of her, but not she of him.

Guess what? He will get into trouble if he expresses exasperation.

After marriage the picture changes

Once she is married, she may not want her breasts touched or to be tongued. She only engaged in erotic sexual activities because it was a part of the dating game, and she was curious to find out how it felt. Now that she has him, the sexual relationship has changed.

Of course, he is baffled and indignant. He enjoyed the dating sexual intercourse they had and expected it to continue.

Feeling justified

When dating, she was grateful for his time, attention, and generosity. Now married, she feels justified in thinking resentful thoughts when he fails to treat her in special ways.

Thus, she thinks and feels that he owes her special treatment. He too may have even promised special treatment during dating.

The same conditions apply to the male as well. He expects the same special treatment that he got when they were dating.

Now that they are married, he doesn't always want to be romantic before intercourse. Since she told him that she enjoys intercourse, he doesn't think that romance is necessary. He is eager to immediately get on with love making without kissing and holding her; he is not thinking affectionately. If she isn't thinking sexually, too, at that moment, sexual frustration is about to begin for both of them. This can be the beginning of love pathology.

The importance of love messages

He would feel more like restraining his urges, showing her some affection and appreciation, if she would say to him something like this:

"I am eager for some long sexy kisses tonight,

dear. Hold me tenderly for several minutes. I

want to feel your affection and your excitement

for me. I want it to grow and grow. I want to become passionate for you."

Instead of this healthy communicative love message, she may tell him,

What Is The Bedroom For?

"Put it away. I am too tired tonight."

There is no excitement, no eager expectation, no joy, on the part of either husband or wife when they think like this.

The tarnished illusions

What one thinks at bedtime can make the difference between an exciting sexual relationship or a boring, frustrating, disappointing one. It could turn into a hate session.

When critical, disappointed thinking of a spouse occurs daily, feelings of admiration and affection gradually diminish and the bedroom becomes a place to avoid.

When daily activities stop sexual thinking and appreciation for a spouse, then the illusion is tarnished. She or he becomes like everyone else.

What further destroys the illusion?

A man and woman usually have different ideas about the purpose of marriage. While dating they talked, seeking to find out if they shared the same ideas of importance in a marriage relationship. Unfortunately, each of them at that time took too many ideas and feelings for granted. Consequently, they didn't ask the right questions. At the day of the wedding, they are duped by the glorious feelings of love into thinking that their ideas for living together are the same.

Marriage success in the bedroom may be adversely affected by what the couple thought the purpose of marriage was while dating.

Why does a woman marry?

What ideas are important enough for a woman to marry a Man?

This varies amongst women.

To one woman, what is particularly important about being married is having a male take care of her.

To another woman, what is particularly important is having two children.

Usually, for a teenage girl, what is particularly important is escaping from mother and father.

To a young woman, it may be the "in" thing to do at the moment, as her female friends are marrying and becoming pregnant. She doesn't want to be left out.

To another woman, intercourse is the most important activity of her existence.

To some women, it is status, power, and financial security.

For other women, sexual intercourse is so related to pregnancy and training a child that their erotic thinking may be limited. Having a child is such an important part of living to these women that they may not think as lustfully or erotically as men do.

Usually, however, it is a combination of these ideas that causes a woman to marry. But when one of these are particularly important, then this can affect what happens in

WHAT IS THE BEDROOM FOR?

the bedroom and the happiness of the marital relationship. A man should know what his woman's idiosyncrasies are.

Men have a stereotype set of ideas or images about women. This guides them in dating and mate selection.

Why does a man marry?

What do men think is important in marriage?

It is mostly sexual thinking.

A man will mentally undress women. Today, with bikinis and other revealing types of attire, he doesn't have to do this. She has already done it for him. If he has seen his sister and/or mother in the nude, he has already seen a nude woman.

While masturbating for years in bed, he has thought about stroking different females whom he has seen on TV, in person, or in periodicals. He may have even thought of having sexual intercourse with his best boyfriend's mother, if she is beautiful and sexy.

I never have known a man to think about creating a baby while masturbating. Most men don't think that way. Their thinking is directed at reaching a climax— that is, ejaculation. They are only thinking about — physical pleasure. They don't like rubbers. If he gets his penis into her, he is apt to go off regardless of whether she gets pregnant or not. And in these days of abortion, he doesn't have to be that concerned with getting her pregnant. Her having an abortion doesn't usually bother him.

51

Many males don't think in terms of pleasure in child development or with rearing children, as they believe this is woman's responsibility and satisfaction. Since he provides the physical care for his wife and children, he thinks he has done his share. What permits him to think only in terms of physical pleasure? Frankly, he is too busy thinking promiscuously and erotically to think of pleasing his family.

It is this kind of thinking that interferes with sexual intercourse between married couples and not dating couples.

It is the failure of the wife not to know that her husband thinks like this.

It is this thinking of the husband that causes their sexual activity in bed not to bind them to each other. His failure to think affectionately during intercourse may also keep him from being close enough to his wife to prevent an affair.

There are many women who do not want to be lustful thinkers! They finds themselves in conflict with their husbands at bedtime as they gradually discover his masturbation thinking and erotic desires.

Millions of women think that this distinction between lustful and non-lustful thinking should be made. Their fathers and the priesthood of the Catholic Church have forced this distinction upon them. They think that lustful feelings interfere with what their husbands should think and feel about them. There is constant controversy over lustful thinking which has existed for centuries and in all kinds of cultures.

WHAT IS THE BEDROOM FOR?

Can excessive erotic thinking in the bedroom cause an affair and end the marriage?

A husband and wife came to my office years ago to talk about their erotic activities. He had mirrors placed on the ceiling and the walls to observe his wife and himself in various sexual acts. Then he made a viewing hole in the wall. He forced his wife to have sexual intercourse with other men so that he could watch this kind of sexual activity. When she could no longer tolerate it, they came to the office, wondering if they could stay together. Love will take a lot of abuse, but not that much. This marriage did end in divorce.

There are prominent individuals, high officials, and many others from all walks of life who engage in wife swapping. It seems to me that it should be called husband swapping. It can't really be called love affairs. Particularly when you draw a name out of a hat and sometimes have three partners in a night. This is lustful thinking acted out.

A love affair in the bedroom is considered an exclusive relationship. The people involved may also have guilty feelings about how they have intercourse.

I remember an M.D. who was employed by a group of wife swappers to protect them against VD. He finally gave up monitoring the group as there was always some member who was discontent. He or she would engage in sexual activities outside the group and then bring VD into the group. Apparently, lustful or masturbation thinking for some individuals gets out of control even though they are a part of a wife swapping group.

53

If you have grasped these two examples, you obviously believe in distinctions between erotic thinking and wholesome thinking. Many of those who engage in these practices believe in protecting children from lustful activities.

To maintain a marriage relationship, to avoid affairs and create emotional security, lustful thinking must be controlled in the bedroom.

The strongest love feelings in the bedroom come from wholesome love thinking.

What everyone should know is that what one thinks in the bedroom makes a difference in married sexual intercourse and marriage stability.

CHAPTER 6

DISSATISFACTION IN THE BEDROOM

For couples, the bedroom can be an exciting, happy place during the dating season.

After the wedding ceremony for millions of couples, the bedroom is not a place for sexual contentment. Sexual dissatisfaction is experienced sometimes, often, or regularly. For thousand of couples it starts on the wedding night. For others, it comes months or years later. This dissatisfaction can be one cause for an affair.

Female complaints

Here are some of the female's continuing complaints and disappointments which can eventually lead to an affair or a divorce.

1. He can't maintain an erection.
2. He may have to wait days to consummate the marriage.
3. He is so fast that she can't enjoy it.
4. He is so rude, rough, and inconsiderate during intercourse that she can't tolerate him. She must regularly initiate the sexual action.
5. He wants oral sex, anal sex, and/or other types of sexual behaviors that offend her.
6. He, after a six months' honeymoon, gets so busy with his law practice, medical practice, business or whatever occupation that he lacks the time to give her personal attention and to enjoy her sexually.

Many wives tell me that their husbands say they are no fun in bed. Out of desperation, these wives talk to women friends, read books and then decide that their husbands are at fault.

To test this conclusion, a wife client of mine picked up a male at a bar. Then they went to a motel and had sexual intercourse. To her surprise, she had a great time in bed with him. The wife discovered it was not her but her husband who could not perform.

This discovery has forced many a wife to choose one of several alternatives — one, live with her husband contentedly although not sexually satisfied; two, get a divorce (if the relationship is too difficult and unhappy); three, continue a series of affairs for practical reasons rather than get a divorce; four, harass her husband in a variety of ways; or five, **teach him how to be a better lover.** These real life situations happen to couples every day.

Male complaints

If the female complaints are shocking, let's listen to some of the male complaints:

1. Some men say that their wife is too modest.
2. She can't climax.
3. She wants a whole hour of lovemaking.
4. It takes her forever to reach a climax.
5. Her period takes ten days.
6. Others say she is so filled with fear at the thought of a penis penetrating her that she tightens her vagina so much he can't slide it in.

DISSATISFACTION IN THE BEDROOM

7. Many times, she thoughtlessly washes her hair, puts it up in curlers, cleanses her skin and takes a bath. All this goes on while he waits for her in bed with an erection. She takes so long to prepare for bed that he finally is out of the mood and angry.

8. She starts a project before bedtime without thinking, either thoughtlessly or deliberately ignoring her husband's sexual needs.

9. She talks on the telephone to a women friend or a relative when she should be in bed. This makes him feel unimportant to her.

10. He goes to pick her up and she inevitably makes him wait, a half hour in the car before she decides to go home.

Men have also told me that while they were having intercourse, their wife talks about cooking or what happened to little Adam that day. He finally loses his erection.

A husband can become so frustrated if this happens often enough that he not only loses his erection for his wife, but he is forced to go elsewhere to be satisfied or is forced to frustrate her. Angry and unsatisfied he is liable to do both.

These are the dissatisfactions which build and mount until it is impossible for a husband to cope. If there are too many of these dissatisfactions night after night, he will be looking for a mistress or thinking about a divorce.

What causes sexual dissatisfaction between men and women?

A primary reason for dissatisfaction in the bedroom is the lack of understanding between couples about the essential social and physical sexual differences, particularly by couples in their twenties.

Most wives, or women, are ignorant about a male's sexual training and his masturbation background which affects a wife's sexual satisfaction or dissatisfaction.

An essential social sexual difference is that a male marries primarily to have sexual intercourse. He expects to engage in it whenever he wants. Because he may have masturbated so much as a boy, a teenager, and a young adult, he is not accustomed to waiting for a woman to get ready or to be in the mood. He gets an erection and is ready. He expects to mount the female and start stroking.

Yes, this is the sexual instinct in all males. Have you ever gone to the zoo, farm or woods to watch the ducks and birds? The male bird is constantly chasing the female, not to kiss and snuggle, but to mount, have sex and be done with her.

Some males don't want to waste time kissing, stroking breasts and legs and talking a lot. An erection demands action.

Too much excitement during sex can cause premature ejaculation

DISSATISFACTION IN THE BEDROOM

An experienced masturbator has learned that the big moment of satisfaction is ejaculation. He has heard that women have a climax, whatever that means. He is not that concerned with her satisfaction, just his own great moment of excitement. For years, he has masturbated by himself without having to consider a women's feelings, body responses and other needs. Many times he develops very selfish feelings in terms of sexual development. He is extremely limited in his interaction with a female. His sexual fantasies get the better of him.

There are husbands who masturbate daily and frequently after intercourse with their wives, much to her disappointment.

A husband can become overly excited anticipating intercourse by mentally undressing women, listening to sexual jokes and watching lustful TV programs. Thus being overly excited before lovemaking with his wife, he immediately ejaculates upon insertion of his penis. Premature ejaculation causes a husband to feel disappointed as he has not had several minutes to get that excited feeling of having his penis inside of his wife's vagina. He knows that she has not had time to enjoy it either. He has disappointed her. He is afraid that she will not let him try again.

When the wife is remiss in expressing her feelings

The wife, on the other hand, who has times during the day may become sexually aroused for him. But she is too embarrassed to telephone to tell him so. These feelings, unfortunately, pass by the time he gets home. She forgets to tell him. He doesn't know that she still has these sexual feelings for him during the day or night.

Why? Something is always interrupting her since she is always on call. He only knows that at night she is too tired. At bedtime she just wants to be held, reassured, kissed, and to feel the strength of his body, which relaxes her.

Being thoughtless, her husband doesn't understand her feelings, nor does he respect her obligations to the family as a whole. This is because he has never had to be concerned with the obligations of the female.

Often a man doesn't understand how a woman's affectionate feelings affect his sexual satisfaction.

Many women marry a man to be admired, held, kissed, and to have someone feel their bodies. They expect flirtatious remarks. Since most women are talkative in petty matters, they expect their men to talk this way to them.

During the dating period, a man finds this kind of talk fun. He wants to marry this woman and desires her sexually so much that he will do anything to please her to get sexual intercourse while dating. This serious misunderstanding, on both their parts, becomes a bone of contention. After marriage, he loses interest in petty talk and in preliminary love procedures while she wants to continue them.

Since she got this attention while dating, she expects it to continue after marriage. She naturally expects the dating game to last. This is a serious misunderstanding many women often make.

DISSATISFACTION IN THE BEDROOM

Sometimes the dissatisfactions are not just sexual, but are due to the personal differences in males and female's lifestyles, personal values, and the lack of skills necessary to maintain a household.

A husband's attention and affection for his wife begins to wane after the first year, usually for the deficiencies he sees in her character: a lack of emotional control, a drug habit, drinking too much, or a lack of knowledge about their many differences. The extent to which his attention and affection for her diminish, increases the risk of an affair or a divorce.

The admiration, the kissing, the flirtatious remarks might have continued on his part if she had been prepared to be a mother and wife by taking courses and practical training; and if he had also been prepared to be a husband and father by taking courses and practical training. Since neither of them is prepared for their role as a wife or husband or as parents, in time, the disappointment and the correction of each other begins. Gradually, there is a diminishing of sexual affection.

Thus begins the sexual and affection conflict between a man and a woman because they start from an entirely different point of view as you have read. She has little or no knowledge of his masturbation thinking or his sexual experiences. He is not really concerned about her feminine desires. Both lack necessary knowledge and training for their married relationships to succeed.

The difference between men and women's conflicts

Her way of going to bed is not his. He doesn't want to engage in pillow talk as some wives would like to do. There is now unhappiness in the bedroom for both of them.

Remember, she wants to be approached romantically. She can't say to him. "Let's go to bed and fuck." This is not lady-like. This is using a bad word. What will he think of her making such an advance? What will God think? Is she to be considered a whore for saying this?

He, unlike her, doesn't have to live with the idea of being a slut or whore. Promiscuity is acceptable for the male, but not for the female.

To prevent a daughter or sister from acting immodestly and initiating a sex act like a streetwalker, a father, brother or other male may call her a slut or whore. They hope that this accusation will hurt her feelings that she will not act in this manner.

An accusation of being a whore restrains a woman from talking sexually or acting immodestly with her husband, although he or she is usually not aware of it.

He knows that she may be offended if he walks up to her and says, "I am angry. We have not had intercourse in the last seven days. When are you going to start putting out again?" He suppresses his anger and resentment.

One doesn't usually hear wives say to their husbands, "For two weeks you have failed to have intercourse with me." They certainly should be able to express their disappointment. After all, why should he be allowed to go thirty days without touching her, much less not having sexual intercourse with her? He is not even apologetic about it. He offers her no explanations. He doesn't have to feel guilty about this, but she does.

Many women and men usually can't talk as husband and wife about their sexual distress and experiences to each other. During their childhood training they were not allowed to express themselves in conversation to their parents or siblings about their sexual needs, information or desires. Not having that freedom as children, it is only natural that they can't speak to each other as adults.

Many women can't talk during lovemaking. They can't tell their husbands what to do or not do. Husbands must guess what wives like. Wives were taught that the fragile male image can't take being told how to have intercourse.

Many times the male can't tell his wife how he is feeling either or it will disturb her mood. They engage in sexual activity silently. They both close their eyes so that they can't see each other; they turn out the lights. I guess they are afraid that they will get caught and scolded if they make a sound.

Maybe this silent sexual activity starts by having sex in the back seat of a car, on a floor or standing up. In the dark it is done without conversation so that the lovers will not be caught. Since most of the sexual words are considered naughty for a child to say, adult couples cannot break this childhood restriction on sexual talk.

If a couple can't talk to each other about sexual intercourse and think of creative ways of solving sexual frustration, they soon become estranged. Then one or the other could be ripe for an affair, an illegal adventure.

Some Catholics can't talk sexually to a spouse in bed, as this comes under the category of lust and carnal knowledge. There are Protestants who think the same way. These couples obviously can't talk to each other either.

Neither Jesus nor Paul told anyone how to rid themselves of lustful thinking. Accordingly, preachers, priests, and rabbis have not been able to rid themselves of lustful thinking in all these many centuries.

If some psychologists or psychiatrists can end lustful thinking, then everyone can enjoy celibacy and the end of the human race. To end lustful thinking would be a sad day for millions of couples who enjoy it.

Fatigue strikes

Another source of sexual dissatisfaction between husbands and wives is fatigue. Her menstruation may causes a natural iron deficiency, which creates fatigue. Many wives have from two to ten days when they can't engage in intercourse because of excessive menstruation. At that time her natural disposition is not to want to engage in strenuous physical activities. Many times this fatigue is accompanied by depression or irritability. These conditions further fatigues her and interferes with both their leisure-time activities and love life.

DISSATISFACTION IN THE BEDROOM

His fatigue doesn't usually interfere with his sexual desires and feelings, so he misunderstands her fatigue — perhaps he thinks that she is trying to avoid him, not interested in his feelings, not wanting to satisfying him, etc. There is now more misunderstanding in the bedroom.

Dr. Wise tells clients who are trying to solve a lack of sexual activity at bedtime, "Why don't you set aside Monday, Wednesday, and Friday nights for romance?" The reaction he heard from them was, "But it is supposed to be spontaneous! You can't do it on a schedule. That makes it so mechanical." With this excuse the couple continues to have a lack of sexual desire and communication for one another.

If wives took a nap at midday in preparation for the most important time in family living (6 to 10 pm), this would boost their energy to have an affectionate relationship with their husbands. Many women with children are working, due to the cultural changes since 1960. Therefore, they can't take a nap. For these women, their energy level remains low.

Men, too, might make the family happier after coming home from a hard day's work, if they took a thirty minute nap before supper. The English custom of dinner at eight has merit.

Waking up forty-five minutes earlier after a good night's rest is also a way to satisfy their sexual desires for each other. Why wait until 11 p.m. when obviously both spouses are too tired to enjoy each other? Some women, however, tend to be late sleepers in the morning, so this is not a welcomed suggestion for them.

CHAPTER 6

Isn't it surprising that the woman or man who have these excuses for not solving sexual frustration can have an affair, engage in all kinds of sexual activities and take care of a family, too?

I guess many spouses think that the promise made at the wedding ceremony will withstand any form of abuse, neglect, lack of attention or affection. Either that, or they are unaware they are adversely affecting their spouse by what they are, or are not doing or saying.

Self-pity can justify any kind of action and can blind spouses to what they are doing to each other.

Sexual frustrations on the part of the husband or wife can build into a desire for another man or woman. Thus, sexual frustration can be the beginning of growing self-pity for one of them, if not both. Many times, there are enough good qualities in each of them to keep them together.

Everyone should understand that sexual dissatisfactions can cause love affairs and diminish married love feelings. If spouses will correct these dissatisfactions promptly, there will be no divorce. There will be only a lasting, satisfying marriage.

CHAPTER 7

GETTING PREGNANT

What excitement there is when a wife announces she is pregnant! Parents of the couple bellow with pride. Grandparents and friends gather together to arrange a shower for the little one. A good feeling can be felt in the household. All share in the couple's joy in anticipation of the new arrival.

But in some instances it can be a big disappointment for some husbands and wives. It will unfortunately, depend on how each of them were nurtured. It can be the first step toward an affair or a divorce. Does this need to happen?

A misunderstanding.

Millions of women want to get pregnant. Hundreds of thousands of men are not excitedly interested in becoming fathers but, for irrational reasons, they enjoy getting a woman pregnant. She mistakenly assumes that her husband's eagerness to get her pregnant is associated with a strong desire to become a father in terms of devoting his time to training a child. How can she make such a serious mistake? Simple. Sometimes, when the couple is having intercourse, he suggests that she get pregnant. By his occasionally talking about the pleasure of having a son, a daughter or both, she naturally thinks that her eager expectation to have a baby is as important to him as it is to her.

He is nurtured to be a vocational success

He, on the other hand, has been nurtured to be a vocational success or at least self-supporting. So he thinks about being a cop, space pilot, engineer, whatever. He has also been encouraged to be interested in basketball, football, sports, crafts and cars, but definitely not babies and children. This is an essential social sexual difference between a man and a woman which may become a source of married love difficulties. Depending upon how they resolve these difficulties, an affair or divorce may happen.

A husband can really be devastated by pregnancy and by a baby, even if he wanted a baby very much. Earning more money suddenly becomes a necessity for him. He never anticipated the disruption in their daily lives that is caused by a baby.

As both their unhappiness and disappointments mount through parenting, the wife may even regret she ever got pregnant or, for that matter, married. Many times an affair, on his or her part, is used as a solution to their misunderstandings of differences in parental expectations.

She is nurtured to be a wife and mother

She either forgets or doesn't understand that she has been nurtured from childhood to be a mother by her mother, sisters, girl friends, other women and males in her life.

In her teens or shortly after marriage, she may have made eager preparations to be a mother by reading books, taking classes, getting child care experience by taking care of children and by informing herself on pregnancy, diets and physical training programs that are necessary for her to have a baby.

If she has expended all these efforts to be a mother, she should know by his lack of the same efforts and by the lack of childhood nurturing experiences that he is probably not ready to be a father. However, if she thinks that none of these nurturing steps are necessary for him to become a parent, she will naturally think that he is ready to be a father. Or, if she experiences little of these nurturing experiences herself, she could easily deceive herself into thinking that he is ready to be a parent, too. When she discovers that he is not ready to be a father, she is disappointed. Many mothers do not prepare themselves for this disappointment.

Every woman should acknowledge that a man has little and usually none of the nurturing experiences that she has had to become a parent. More than likely he is not prepared to get her pregnant if he lacks the essential nurturing experiences, in spite of what he says to her during sexual intercourse.

For many males and females, the unfortunate by product of sexual intercourse is a baby. Modern contraception and abortion have been a blessing to many men and women. These procedures, however, pose emotional and ethical questions for her that do not beset him. This is an essential social sexual difference between them.

CHAPTER 7

Dissatisfactions for many couples begin with pregnancy.

The fears associated with pregnancy are in conflict with the desire to get pregnant and presents a contradiction for the woman. Not so for the male. He doesn't have to be afraid of death, pain, unattractive appearances or the fear of falling and hurting the baby, etc. Many times he is unaware of her pregnancy fears and does not give her the emotional support she needs. If he fights and quarrels with her during the days of pregnancy, she may turn to others for understanding and support, but hopefully not another man. Many men are not in any way prepared to emotionally support a wife through the beginning stages of motherhood.

Anything can happen

Until the time of pregnancy, she can engage in sexual activities at any time; the bedroom can be a happy place for them. When the wife becomes pregnant, if she has a husband who has no idea how to support her through this delicate time, it can be an unhappy experience as anything can happen. She can have a threatened abortion. This can stop sexual intercourse and cause him as well as her additional hardships and emotional strain.

The obstetrician may suggest that there be no sexual intercourse in the last month of pregnancy and for a few weeks after delivery. If this is a three month period of sexual abstinence, a male can be unhappy at times because he is forced to refrain from sexual activities.

Some men may engage in a little sexual activity with another woman during this time of pregnancy. Amazing how many women are ready to take advantage of another woman's difficult time. As for the man cheating, yes, he is wrong, but his selfishness and nurturing experiences such as they are allow him to cheat with no conscience. After all he doesn't love the neighbor or girlfriend, he just wants to be sexually satisfied — thereby justifying his actions.

The self-pity of some men

The self-pity of some expectant fathers causes them to have illicit sex, not love. They justify it by saying, "It is sexual urgency." There is no doubt that there is some urgency, which could have been solved by masturbation.

Why some men feel sexual self-pity: remember, their masturbation experiences may have caused them to think selfishly about sexual intercourse and were probably never taught to be sexually considerate of a woman.

Fortunately, other men were taught by their mothers and fathers to be considerate of women and their needs. Some were even expected to help with the household chores. They may have even changed diapers and fed a baby brother or sister. You can be sure, this will be a happy time for both husband and wife.

Baby brings changes

Soon after the baby is born, the woman's attitude changes from being sort of a mistress or a date to her husband to being a mother. She is now responsible for a human life as most women want to be. The helplessness of baby makes mother aware of her responsibilities. There are always the baby's needs to knock her out of the mood for sexual intercourse.

She is always busy bathing, feeding and putting the baby to sleep at night. While she is doing this, she also must feed her husband and herself, clean the kitchen, and do whatever else needs to be done to make the family comfortable. She forgets, at times, that her husband is getting an erection and desires her.

Finally, when she gets to bed, often quite exhausted, she would rather sleep. He gets angry. After all, why did he get married — to have her take care of a baby? No way! It was to take care of him sexually and his other needs. How dare she put him second!

As the baby gets older and a second child is conceived, she gets even busier after dinner taking care of the babies and the household duties. She necessarily neglects her husband by a lack of attention, affection and probably sex.

Remember, he doesn't really want to be a father that much, so he doesn't help out. He doesn't share these parenting experiences with her and drops out as a parent to his detriment. He, at times, becomes resentful of her parenting activities with baby and of household chores. He is unwilling to give her any moral support or help with household chores.

He could be also following male traditions from the cultural era that ended with World War I. The work schedules of men for that era didn't always permit a father to participate in family activities. Men in those days worked five to six days a week and many times ten hours a day. It was physically impossible for the husband to do more than come home, eat dinner, and go to bed.

Some mothers don't want their husbands to be a parent. For whatever reason, they want to be the only parent. No wonder the husband becomes resentful if he does want to be a parent. This attitude can cause an affair.

Some causes of marital disagreements

If the child or children become troublemakers, father, who has no preparation for this can get quite annoyed and critical of his wife.

If father has an overwhelming interest in his occupation at the time of pregnancy and early infancy, there can be marital disagreements about his non-interest in the new born baby making mother feel deserted.

If there is serious illness at the time of pregnancy and during infancy, some husbands can't cope with it. Others just become overwhelmed, irritable, angry and resentful. He may not support his wife emotionally or lend a helping hand with household chores. This can cause severe emotional damage to their relationship, sometimes irreparable.

On the other hand, though, some husbands are great at helping out in times of serious physical illness.

The selfish husband generally blames his wife for the lack of attention. Frankly, he just can't cope. If he has no one to help him understand what his wife is going through during a difficult time of adjustment to a new infant, he may exaggerate his difficulties with his wife to get extra kissing, sympathy and just maybe a little sex. If this doesn't work, he may, in fact, decide to have an illicit affair and tells his new lover, "She never gives me any attention. She is always on the telephone and never stays at home. I don't know what she does all day long."

Fortunately, in many situations there are wives, friends and relatives who will talk to the husband to help him understand the adjustment his wife is making in handling a new born who cannot help himself. She needs to give the infant all the attention he needs at this time and her husband needs to help her. This is when he begins to understand what his wife is going through. He may even learn to help her with the infant and, in doing so, learns to appreciate and love the little infant. He then forms an attachment and becomes the proud father instead of the selfish husband. The husband grows emotionally and spiritually and forgets all about an affair when family and friends help him to see past his ego.

During their wife's pregnancy, most men do not receive the information and help they need from medical doctors, clergymen and others on how to become good fathers and caring husbands. Who then is left to help them? Obviously, another woman.

It is important that everyone know that the time to prevent married love difficulties (an affair), is at the time of pregnancy. If love is to be everlasting between a husband and a wife, they must come to understand the emotional stresses of pregnancy and of rearing a child. They must forgive each other's failures during these years.

CHAPTER 8

TOLERATION IS LIKE A RUBBER BAND

Toleration of a spouse's offending behavior is the elasticity of affection. It is what makes love last. It is like a rubber band. As long as it is not stretched too far, it will snap back to normal but if stretched too far, it will break.

Offending behaviors

Listed here are some of the offending behaviors in personal relationships that can become too intolerable for one or both spouses to resolve:

1. At the time of the marriage, one or both were not really in love. This can be a secret or known fact at the time or may be revealed later during the marriage.

2. Not knowing what good human relationships are or if one spouse knows but refuses to practice them, the marriage relationship gradually deteriorate.

3. One or both are promiscuous.

4. The parent-child relationship is too difficult for one spouse or both spouses.

5. Excessive self-pity and injustice collecting.

6. The male wants a mother for a wife.

7. The female wants a parent's love from a husband. She wants to be the irresponsible member.

8. Addiction to alcohol, drugs, food, or cigarettes.

9. Neurotic behavior, severe anxiety, depression, excessive hostility, severe dependency, severe humiliation, or severe anger.

10. Physical illness of a chronic nature.

11. Workaholic.

12. Chronic unemployment, although the spouse is skilled and capable of employment.

13. Sexual deviations or inadequate sexual development.

14. Failure to recognize the difference between dating love and married love.

15. A lack of etiquette.

There can be any number of combinations of these intolerable conditions.

There is a group of spouses whose personal relationships are good, but who enter into illicit love affairs because of sexually intolerable conditions.

Another group of spouses whose personal sexual relationships are good enter into illicit affairs because they cannot control their sexual desires for other men or women. These men are interested in sexual excitement, not love. As long as this can be done secretly, the marriage can last for years. Once the promiscuity is known, it usually becomes an intolerable condition.

When both spouses are promiscuous, and not jealous, promiscuity is a tolerable condition for them. These spouses may belong to spouse swapping clubs.

What makes a behavior intolerable?

Innumerable repetitions of acts and/or criticisms that are unreasonable and inconsiderate, such as;

if a person won't change irritating behaviors;

if a person's sense of fair play is extremely violated;

if there is a lack of appreciation for the other spouse's efforts and or;

if anger, disappointment, depression and belittlement are expressed at the same time, then any one of these factors, or any combination thereof can make a relationship intolerable.

Intolerableness is an overwhelming feeling of helplessness. In other words, as long as the other spouse is fair, willing to change, appreciative and expresses positive feelings, the difficulties can be tolerated.

How long does it take for a condition or fault to become intolerable enough to permit an affair?

The amount of time that faults can be endured varies tremendously, from weeks to months to years. The following reasons explain why it varies. The determination of a spouse to be successful has much to do with it.

1. If a spouse has come from a divorced family, he or she may be more or less determined to make the marriage succeed. Many are more determined not to expose their children to the stress of divorce and step-parents.

2. If the person is committed to winning in general, he or she will expend more effort to succeed.

3. If a spouse's religious training does not permit divorce or affairs, their toleration of the other's faults can last until death parts the couple.

4. If a wife can't earn a living and is a fearful individual, she may tolerate physical beatings and unbelievable conditions.

Emotionally dependent

Husbands or wives, who are so emotionally dependent upon their spouse or who are convinced that no other woman or man could love them, will endure extremely intolerable conditions. In some cases, the toleration may as well be classified as divorce — they occupy separate bedrooms, they talk very little to each other, and there is little or no sexual intercourse.

One male client, several years ago, had a wife who had been in a car accident. Her power to reason and ability to walk had been severely diminished. Due to her helplessness, she had to have nursing care twenty-four hours a day. He was attentive to her for years and had no intention of divorcing her. It was amazing to witness this man's toleration of an intolerable condition.

When does a spouse know that toleration or love is about to end?

There are usually warning signals. It rarely happens suddenly. The inability to cope with a frustrating behavioral pattern is usually expressed, except for the grin and bear it type.

The longer an intolerable condition goes uncorrected, the more the anxiety mounts until there are threats of all kinds such as:

"I am going to move out."

"I will get a lover."

"I will hit you."

"I am going to cut off your allowance and your credit cards."

"I am going to commit suicide.

"I can't stand this much longer."

A most serious warning is when the frustrated spouse complains to outsiders about the offending spouse or offenders (children, in-laws or anyone else living in the house) to hopefully seek help in creating a more comfortable environment for himself or herself. This call for help, a real danger signal, is a strong indication that toleration is about to end.

Occasionally, there is no warning. The silent suffering spouse just sneaks off. The vocal spouse is shocked and rightfully complains, "But you never voiced your complaints."

If the offending spouse doesn't improve his or her ways, the other spouse, instead of resorting to an affair or a divorce, may become just a chronic complainer until death. This is tough on both of them.

After hearing innumerable complaints, threats, and experiencing occasional violent actions, why doesn't the offending spouse recognize the seriousness and change the offending behavior patterns? Since toleration by the abused spouse has lasted for months or years, the offending spouse is deceived into thinking that there is no urgency to change. Since neither the complainer nor the offender spouse makes any records or logs of the number of complaints, they do not realize or recognize the necessity to change. Both become accustomed to cycling the complaints, with occasional over-reactions when the tension becomes too severe.

Why correct offending behavior

Many spouses will not correct an offending behavior if it is not serious. For any number of ridiculous reasons, the complaining spouse can't tolerate the behavior.

The dating experience causes the offending spouse to think that he or she doesn't have to change.

Dating couples mislead each other by saying, "I love you the way you are." After many years of parental training and critical remarks from teachers, children, and teenagers, these are welcomed words from a lover. Why not keep such an admirer for a lifetime? After hearing your dating lover tell you how wonderful you are many times, it is difficult to believe that one's offending actions are going to endanger a future marriage. Supposedly, the well of affection and toleration never runs dry. Most every parent has been taught this truth and, in turn, teaches it to their children.

There is also the betrothal promise that says no change is necessary. The words "for better or for worse, for richer for poorer, in sickness and in health, until death do us part" guarantee that no change is necessary. As immature and inexperienced as most couples are at the time of the first marriage, this really is an unreasonable statement. There is a great need for self-improvement and change for about seventy percent of the couples.

Why did the future spouse tolerate offending behavior?

The future spouse may not have been aware of the offending behavior patterns due to the limited social nature of the dating relationship. Or the future spouse didn't experience it often enough to be vexed. A person in love is usually oblivious to the idea that the lover has behavior problems that he or she can't tolerate.

The parents of one of the dating partners, if asked, could have told the other dating partner of the annoying behavior patterns of their son or daughter. They could have told the spouse-to-be that they could not convince their son or daughter that their behavior was irritating and unnecessary.

However, in the offending spouse's mind, he justifies his position believing that if a parent tolerated his or her behaviors for eighteen years, certainly a wife or husband can too.

This is why one must ask the right questions or seek professional assistance during the dating period, as it generally takes daily living to surface intolerable conditions or faults. Dating couples usually ignore parents. One reason is that neither partner wants their faults known. Another reason is the fear of parental disapproval of his or her lover. I hope all lovers will now be aware of the failure of love when stretched and stressed too much over offending behavior and seek assistance.

Part III - The Affair

CHAPTER 9

THE WEAKNESSES OF THE LOVE AFFAIRS

While an affair is usually a triangle, it can beget a chain of affairs.

A variety of affairs

Years ago, a client arrived in my office for his first appointment. He confessed that he was having an affair but really did not want to divorce his wife. He asked if I would please talk to his mistress? I consented.

During his mistress' appointment, she told me that she had another lover and that she didn't want my client to know. Then she asked if I would mind talking to her second lover, as she is thinking of marrying him.

After my appointment with the mistress, my first client, the husband, had a second appointment in which he revealed he was bisexual and wanted me to talk to his boyfriend. So he was having sexual relations with his wife, a mistress and a male.

As if I didn't have enough complications, my client's wife also called for an appointment. She revealed to me that she had a lover. She then asked, "Is my husband talking to you because he found out I have a lover?" I, of course, replied, "No." She then decided to become a client.

My next surprise was that the wife's lover decided he also needed an appointment.

Needless to say, I had appointment difficulties and didn't dare let any of these individuals arrive at my door at the wrong moment. By now it may be obvious why there were so many affairs. The fact, that the husband was bisexual probably had caused them.

I remember one wealthy mistress, past forty, who offered me a large sum of money if I would help her marry one of my clients, a single man in his fifties. She made the appointment without his knowledge. No, I didn't take the money, only for therapy sessions, and told her I could not guarantee her any such thing. The reason being, it would depend upon many issues for both of them. She decided to see me anyway.

No, they didn't get married. He was happily having affairs with other women that she didn't know about. She had thought he was committed to her and their affair lasted about four years. They had fun. Neither was married.

Sometimes a lover passes his mistress along to a friend. They may share her for awhile. It is not uncommon for two female friends to share a male sexually, sometimes in the same bed.

What surprises everyone is an affair at the time of the wedding ceremony. The bride may be pregnant by one man, but marries another. These usually are all single individuals.

Is the mistress always a stranger?

My clients have taught me that the mistress is frequently the wife's best friend. Sometimes she lives next door. I may then have three of them for clients, but rarely all four. The best friend frequently loses out.

The Weaknesses Of The Love Affairs

As one might suspect, the husband's secretary or a woman who is working with him daily can frequently be the other woman.

Why is the lover someone close to the husband or wife, rather than a stranger?

The best friend is privy to confidential information of both spouses, especially if she lives next door.

The wife tells her best friend that her husband is great in bed, but not much good for anything else. The wife's best friend knows better. She knows that the wife isn't that easy to live with. If the best friend is disappointed with her husband and has been thinking about a divorce, but has not discussed it with anyone, she can see and hear that the wife's husband is a far better catch than her own. The wife, on the other hand, has no idea about her best friend's plans and feels confident about her husband's loyalty. The best friend waits for the opportunity to create a love relationship with the wife's husband. If she lives ten feet away, she has a real advantage.

One day there is a big fight between the husband and wife. The opportunity has arrived. She takes sides with the husband. Now he has an alliance, and she is convenient — next door. At the right moment she encourages an embrace and a kiss. They may have already been exchanging friendly kisses as neighbors or friends for a couple of years.

Another example is when the wife innocently reveals to her husband that her best friend is really sexy and unhappily married. In this case, the husband may initiate a romance at a New Year's Eve or other type party. A little hand holding and kissing can go further than was intended by the best friend and husband. On this occasion, the best friend may have an affair and get pregnant by the neighbor's husband. In the days before abortion, this was a very difficult situation to resolve. Today, with legal abortion, the difficulty can be more easily resolved if it is an accidental pregnancy with no love involved, just alcohol.

A man's secretary has the same opportunity that his wife's best friend has. She works with him every day. She knows his kids. She knows the wife. She also is privy to many intimate details. She frequently knows from conversations with her boss that he really is displeased with his wife. She knows, too, that his complaints are legitimate. She can wait for the right moment. It will come.

Cardinal facts can lead to an affair

Cardinal facts are the primary intimate knowledge of a person and should be kept confidential between husband and wife, especially if a marriage is fragile. When cardinal facts become known, another person may consciously or unconsciously think there is justification to become involved in a love triangle. The following three cardinal facts can lead to an affair:

1. Being close to one or both spouses and aware of marital disagreements;

2. Being privy to a lot of intimate knowledge about the spouses; and

3. Being single and unhappy or married and unhappy with his or her spouse.

The Weaknesses Of The Love Affairs

The sharing of self-pity

In almost all love triangles there is the sharing of self-pity. Either the husband or wife says, "I am so unhappy with my spouse." The other person says, "I know just what you mean." Then they share their injustices together. They begin to become attracted to each other as they share their unhappiness. They no longer feel alone and misunderstood. There is someone who understands, someone to lend emotional support. They enjoy their miseries together. Before long they start kissing and holding hands. Then one day it happens! They become so happy in sharing their unhappiness that they fall in "love," and have sex. They have such a great time that they decide to do it again. At this time, generally, there is no idea of divorce or marriage — just fun sneaking away together. Usually it is sexual fun.

Severe marital differences

Sometimes an affair starts because of severe differences between husband or wife's parenting. The husband is unhappy over the way his wife is rearing the children, or vice versa.

He makes suggestions to her. She doesn't listen to him nor does she accept his advice. After all, these are her children. She gradually shuts him out of the parenting role. He feels rejected and begins to complain to others.

There is always a woman around looking for a man who is interested in rearing children. Another woman quickly zeros in on him. After all, her husband has no interest in their children and is not much good in bed either. She has found the perfect step-father for her children as they both have mutual parenting interests. He is lonely and accepts her children. Soon they are holding hands and sharing miseries and lovers' feelings. "Oh, it feels so good to have someone with the same ideas about raising children and parenting them together," they tell me.

Then one night they get into bed together. She enjoys sex with him. Now, she knows she has found the lover she wants. The affair flourishes. It is time for two divorces.

Married to a workaholic

Then there is a woman who is married to a workaholic. He is gone most of the time. All he wants out of the marriage is sex three times a week and a little orgy on the weekend. The sexual relationship is excellent.

All she must do to keep him happy is run errands, wash clothes, and not mind his playing golf on Saturday. She prepares about six meals a week for him. An easy stint, except as a wife, she essentially lives alone. When the loneliness gets to be too much for her and she feels sufficiently used, she may be ready for an affair.

A special category

Traveling salesmen, airline pilots, and military officers fall into a special category as they are gone from home so much. Some of them like to have a little sexual adventure when away from home. They have no intention of getting a divorce. They just want a little excitement and diversion. As long as they can keep their overnight affairs a secret, all is fine.

The Weaknesses Of The Love Affairs

Some women enjoy this kind of married life with the husband gone much of the time.

Other wives cannot cope with the absence. It is not that they miss their husbands, but they are afraid to be alone at night. After awhile they may find a lover who likes to stay at home and be more of a family man.

The young mistresses

There are always the teenage girls and women in their early twenties who have affairs to get away from home. They sometimes become mistresses to married men. Such female clients frequently do not want to be an adult woman. They only want to remain ten- or sixteen-year-old girls with adult privileges. Their mothers encouraged them to grow up, but they resist. These females are so unhappy with the family pressure to grow up that any male seems okay to them, especially someone with assets.

Other teenage girls and women in their early twenties want big homes, expensive cars, travel, and entertainment. All it takes for them to get it are kisses and hugs and time in bed, which they enjoy. They figure, why not go for it? Why not accept this carefree, happy existence of being a mistress to a successful man. If she can have a maid to take care of the house, her own car, lots of clothes in the closet and meals out with possibly an offer of marriage, why not? She doesn't need to take care of anyone. He only wants a baby doll, she thinks. Since any male is okay, some of them do marry. Before long, they discover the husbands are not okay, especially if they expect their wives to grow up and keep house and/or become a mother. These young mistresses or wives become terribly disappointed and many cannot survive this type relationship and end it in divorce or annulment.

When a husband or wife is severely disappointed and realizes that their marriage is not going to improve, one of them may start an affair or file for a divorce, especially if they are married to one of the following types of individuals.

Married to a severely depressed person

Many times a wife or husband who marries a severely depressed person cannot cope with their spouse's condition and may become involved in an affair. How a depressed individual ever gets married is a mystery. My guess is that during dating love he or she escaped depression long enough to deceive the innocent mate. This kind of extreme depression should be treated by a psychotherapist. If this is all that is wrong, the affair can end if the depressed spouse seeks therapy and responds to it. This marriage can be saved.

Married to a severely neurotic person

There are spouses who are having affairs because they are married to a man or a woman who suffer from severe anxiety neuroses. Neurotic spouses are difficult to live with. They are moody. They can be quarrelsome, critical, have temper tantrums, phobias, depressions, and be excessive eaters, drinkers or drug users. They can also be funny, witty, clever, enthusiastic, curious, entertaining, or talented.

If one or both spouses are neurotic, they should employ a psychologist to train them out of their neurotic behavior. Love by a spouse will not conquer a neurosis. In this way, they can learn how to rear children and how to take care of a household successfully with or without servants. These marriages may not end in divorce. The excitement and affection of living with a person like this is sometimes worth the roller coaster ride for someone who has nothing better to do. Perhaps by understanding their neurotic behavior, they can learn to live sensibly together.

Affairs turned into a marriage

When an affair is based on sincere love, affection, character and stability (which is rare), these individuals can turn their love affair into a marriage. They do live happily ever after.

Psychotherapy, not love

Two thirds of married couples need some psychotherapy at one time or another during marriage to correct misunderstandings they may be experiencing to save their marriage and to bring peace and harmony back into their lives.

A third of the nation's married population needs extensive psychotherapy if one or both of the spouses are neurotic or psychotic.

Unfortunately, most men and women who are seeking a mate are unaware that there are so many individuals in need of either some therapy or extensive therapy. They also don't believe or know that psychotherapy is the only answer, not love.

Affairs not based on real love

Self-pity and sexual attraction, usually the basis for an affair, are not the right reason to get a divorce. It is important that everyone understand that many affairs are not based on real love. By understanding the various causes of an affair one can either avoid it, manage it better, or successfully conclude it. Psychotherapy can help untangle the mess and intolerable feelings the couple has for one another.

Dissolving illicit affairs

Believe it or not, an illicit affair can usually be dissolved within ninety days. What most individuals don't know is that most affairs are not based on love, but on sympathy and/or self-pity and/or sexual attraction. The illicit lovers are somewhat aware it is not real love, too. Psychologists can and have broken up many love affairs based on the wrong reasons and the misinterpretations of husband and wife. Many marriages can be saved if couples initially prepare themselves for marriage.

CHAPTER 10

IS SECRECY NECESSARY?

Secrecy is considered a necessary part of creating a love relationship, legal or illegal. Every lover practices it to some extent. Misrepresentation is a form of secrecy. Lovers often practice acceptable forms of deception and enjoy it.

Acceptable forms of secrecy

Women practice secrecy constantly but especially when dating. They use cosmetics, falsies. They pick clothes that hide physical features that are considered unattractive or that accentuate desirable features. For dating purposes they contrive settings in which they feel comfortable. They make false statements to create a favorable impression. For centuries, women often disguised their intelligence to help the male feel superior.

Men practice secrecy, too. They will borrow a friend's car or rent one to impress a woman. They will take her to places they don't care about just to make a good impression. If they are serious about her, they will dress up to create an even better impression. They will use exaggerated statements to flatter her. Like women, they will do anything to conceal their faults.

Hiding faults and exaggerating good qualities are a regular part of the dating process.

Non-acceptable forms of secrecy

Other forms of misrepresentation or secrecy, however, are not considered acceptable in love relationships. After marriage, the code changes.

Secret, illicit love affairs are always not acceptable. Men and women out for a little sport sex conceal the fact that they are married. They take off their wedding rings to have a night of fun. When found out, the single women are justifiably angry, while the single men usually resent it, but enjoy the game.

Married men and women know the rules most single individuals obey — "I don't fool around with married people." Knowing this, they then pretend to be single.

Some married individuals who are only out to fool around don't want to deceive another married person. They know this might be harmful and dangerous to that person's marriage, so they go after the unwed individual. The single individual is different; he or she can't be hurt, the married person mistakenly thinks.

Conversely, some single individuals will date married individuals feeling they are safe. They don't have to be concerned about getting married or falling in love. They just want a good time.

Is Secrecy Necessary?

Illicit lovers obviously practice secrecy. Why?

In the case of the male dating spouse, his sexual desire, his self-pity and his attempt to justify injustices so severely blind him to the point that he cannot control himself. He also cannot feel the hurt of another person. He does not want to pay the price for his complaints about his spouse or his sexual desire, so he sneaks. Confident that he can outwit his spouse by sneaking, he fails to ask himself questions about the consequences of infidelity. He feels justified in having an affair to relieve a painful marital relationship. He also seeks the curiosity and the excitement an affair provides.

Why the dishonesty

Deception on the part of one lover, if not both, is sufficient reason for secrecy. By watching the 'secrecy game' being played by clients, I have observed almost always that the cheater gets cheated.

Sometimes the spouse is not seeking a love relationship, but only seeking to find out if he or she is a capable sex partner. This spouse is playing double secrecy and doesn't want the other spouse to know he or she is having an affair. But the testing spouse also doesn't want the lover to know that this is the only reason for the relationship. The lover is being used. Frequently, however,, the lover blindly believes that he or she has not been deceived when the relationship ends even though there is never another date.

The dishonesty is justified by the experimenting spouse on the grounds that the lover had fun. Also, the spouse assumed that the lover must have had sexual intercourse with others, so no harm was done. The experimenting spouse found out what he or she needed to know and justifies the experiment pleading, "There was no other way for me to find out whether my spouse was correct in saying that I am a lousy lay."

What happens now?

What happens to the husband and wife relationship after this kind of a secret relationship occurs? Several solutions are possible.

The spouse who discovers that he or she is sexually inadequate can continue the marriage with this knowledge or can seek sexual therapy or file for a divorce.

Conversely, the experimenting spouse who discovers that he or she is sexually adequate, now knows the accusing spouse is the one who is a lousy lay. With this knowledge, the adequate spouse can either seek therapy for them both, seek a divorce, or teach the offending spouse to be a better lover.

A variety of secret love affairs

There are other kinds of secret love affairs and other reasons for secrecy.

Another kind of secret affair occurs when the male spouse knows that his marriage can only be maintained if he has an occasional love affair on the side. In this case, a variety of secret lovers are used to maintain the marriage. There is little concern for the welfare of the secret 'lovers' who are being used for this purpose.

Is Secrecy Necessary?

Still another kind of secret affair can occur in a marriage, even if the sexual relationship is excellent between the spouses. Sometimes one of them has never had sexual intercourse with another person and wonders if he or she has missed something by being only with one partner. This spouse has a temporary affair to satisfy that curiosity. Usually, after an affair or two, the curious spouse is then satisfied that the married relationship is better or that nothing has been missed.

Many times an affair can and does save a marriage as I have witnessed in my practice.

Avoiding Emotional Conflicts

The spouse who is contemplating whether to end the marriage may have a secret affair. To avoid the emotional scene (moving out, upsetting the children, alimony, child support, sharing accumulated wealth 50-50, attorney's fees, losing friends and relatives, etc.), this unsatisfied spouse secretly dates and justifies this behavior by thinking, "Why upset the family until I am certain I want a divorce?" This spouse is trying to protect the family from any stressful situations that might be unnecessary since there is no certainty at this point whether a divorce will occur.

The woman who has decided to end her marriage may secretly date and shop around amongst eligible males until she finds a new partner suitable for her to remarry. She is truly engaged in secret dating. She knows that she likes sexual intercourse and that she does not wish to go without it for any length of time. She wants to be sure that she has an excellent sexual partner as her husband is a disappointment. If she remarries a wealthy man, she may plan to relieve her husband of all financial responsibility. Then she engineers a divorce. The same can be true for the male. When he finds a right mate, he may try to avoid as much emotional conflict as possible to his spouse and children. There may be no child custody or visitation rights. Because the spouses did intend to marry new partners, this kind of illicit dating is only partially dishonest.

Dishonesty exists as long as a husband or wife is being deceived. When he or she knows the truth, the dishonesty ceases. This is how some wives or husbands protect their family through secrecy until a resolution to a failed marriage can be found.

Some affairs happen accidentally

All affairs do not start as an act of deception, some happen accidentally. At first, there may be no dishonesty in the relationship — but later, yes there is.

Let's say a husband, who is constantly on the go, keeps asking a male friend to chaperon his wife and kids to entertainment events. The wife and children enjoy this entertainment and satisfactory relationship. The wife begins to ask her husband if it is all right for the friend to take her and the children to other events — these chaperoned events happen more and more often. They are all comfortable with one another. They unintentionally form a real attachment to each other. In time, an affair can begin accidentally.

Is Secrecy Necessary?

What can happen to a wife who is constantly busy with clubs and activities, or who is too busy with a career? If the husband and children learn to get along without her, they cease to depend upon her and she is no longer important in their lives. Accidentally the husband may strike up a friendship with another woman who likes and pays attention to him and his children — an affair may begin. Somehow the children and the father never seem to mention her to the wife. There is sort of an unintentionally planned conspiracy.

Then there is the accidental affair that begins when a spouse expresses unhappiness about the marital relationship to another person of the opposite sex. The other person expresses sympathy. In time, both of them look forward to their daily sharing of misery and continued expressions of sympathy which happen more and more frequently. As the need to share misery and sympathy grows, the sexual attraction for each other also grows. Soon they are looking forward to the growing understanding they are experiencing. They enjoy sharing unhappy experiences and unhappiness together. In time, they think they are in love. Blissfully, they decide to divorce their spouses and marry each other. They live happily thereafter sharing miseries.

Drawbacks to secret dating

If one is seeking a new spouse while married, secret dating may be the worst possible solution. There are many drawbacks to secret dating .

Unfortunately, secrecy, by its very nature, places a higher value on sexual relationships and not on social relationships. Besides one can't find out important information from others as to the character of the new lover. Secret dating couples can't go to parties, musical events, visit relatives where others can express their judgment of the future spouse or even enjoy hobbies together. Usually, it is having a tryst at a motel, sneaking a trip out of town, sitting in a car in a remote spot, or calling on the phone.

Secrecy is betrayal of a legal obligation. It is a violation of a very personal promise. If the other person has played fair and fulfilled his or her role as a spouse, this, then is most unfair.

Secret dating, if carried on for years, has serious repercussions on family members. Children's friendships and sporting activities are seriously interrupted. Secrecy may also deny your child the religious training that he or she wants.

Secret dating is not the way to select a mate for a second or third marriage. This is going about it like a thief in the night.

Secrecy and secret dating are pathological forms of love. Everyone should know this.

CHAPTER 11

IS AN AFFAIR FUN?

Sometimes an affair starts with love at first sight. Immediately, both people feel excited and exhilarated. They feel a high. Both of them feel a rush of sexual desire. They want to talk and talk. They can't get enough of each other. They can't bear being separated despite being married to others. They are compelled to see each other. They may never have felt this way before.

He and she wake up in the morning singing, "Oh, what a beautiful morning. Oh, what a beautiful day! I have a wonderful feeling, every thing's going my way." They don't want to walk. They want to skip and whistle. They want to dance, dance, all night. Oh what a glorious feeling.

Regardless of how it starts or how happy they are, then comes 'reality.'

For her, it is the kids, the shopping, the Brownie meetings or the dentist appointments.

For him, it is how to find time to see her.

Complications begin.

There are the managed phone calls. These are easy. But it is the touching and holding that is difficult. If he is a professional man or a salesman, he can find time for a luncheon meeting where they will be able to look at each other, hold hands and kiss. There are the meetings she can skip in the evenings. There is the Saturday golf that he can skip. There is a real awkwardness in meeting but the excitement, the joy, is worth it.

As the fervor mounts, there is the temptation to write. Letters must be hidden. When a husband or wife is not around, these can be read again and again to feel the high.

Letters are dangerous. More affairs have been exposed by letters than anyone will ever know. Usually it is her letters that expose the situation. Men are more apt to discard letters or hide them in a filing cabinet or a drawer at the office.

It is the secrecy! It is the fear of being caught that begins to disturb the relationship. The doubt creeps in as the affection continues to grow. Marriage is obviously becoming a conscious desire.

Now, the reality crashes through. They may say to themselves, "Am I ready to pay the price for this relationship? Will my children like my lover? What will my friends think? How can I face the preacher, the priest or the rabbi? Whom can I share these doubts and concerns with? Who can I trust? Should I have sexual intercourse? If I start, can I stop?"

Now the fun, the excitement of the relationship begins to ebb. Fear, self-judgment and doubt are creeping in.

If the female lover is married with children or if she is single, she begins to pressure her lover for a commitment. Suddenly, for him, too, the fun and the excitement begins to diminish.

IS AN AFFAIR FUN?

He becomes worried and may ponder, "What is he to tell his lover? Is she that great? Is she worth the alimony, the child support, the loss of half of his assets? Does he want another child?" If he is much older, the fear creeps in, can he keep her?

If they are discovered, there are the threats and the accusations of spouses and relatives. It can become a miserable situation.

If the affair is consummated in marriage, then comes the visitation weekends. Her kids visit them. His kids are a problem. This may have been one of the reasons for the divorce. Now she has four kids to comfort and counsel. The ex-spouses harass them. Relatives and friends sit in judgment.

Many times lovers accuse each other of a lack of loyalty. Demands are made. Anger replaces affection. Doubts are rampant. The fun of the affair may now turn into depression. Paradise is lost.

For many remarrying couples, there are painful regrets.

Her ex-husband remarries. He soon is financially better off. He gets along great with his new wife. All the wishes and the expectations that he had with his first wife are fulfilled with his second wife.

The first wife may say to herself, "Was I really the cause of our unhappiness?" This thought occasionally haunts her. "Was the affair worth it?"

Many times this is also true for the first husband's ex-wife.

The fun of the affair and second marriage can then turn into another divorce.

Everyone who starts an affair should think about this kind of ending. Not everyone walks off into the sunset holding hands.

Chapter 12

How Successful Is Secret Dating?

When dating is secret, no one knows how many affairs result in divorce or help a marriage succeed or provoke suicide or just end. The question is how does one measure the success of dating — secret or not?

How is secret dating measured?

Since secret dating is similar to dating before marriage, does one use the same measure of success?

Is success measured by an engagement or a wedding ring?

Is it measured by the number of dates?

Is dating a growth process?

Is having sexual intercourse a part of dating?

Do these same questions apply to secret daters as they do to singles?

No one knows truly how to measure dating success of any kind.

Dating and secret dating develops in the same way and has the same difficulties.

There are the same anxieties and frustrations in beginning and maintaining the relationship.

There are the same fears that it may break up.

There are the same hopes that it will result in marriage (the prize that most desire).

If one of the secret daters does not want to continue dating, then breaking up is just as difficult as it is for the unwed individual.

When a love affair is over, in secret dating or in singles dating, one of the lovers may explain to the other why it must end. Many times the rejected lover refuses to accept these explanations.

In either singles or secret dating, the lover who is breaking away usually has had the fun, the good times and doesn't want to hurt the other lover.

Sometimes a secret love affair ends in marriage because the rejecting lover cannot walk away feeling the depression of the lover. Is this considered a success, or a failure?

I have told clients that I could break up a secret affair within thirty to sixty days. That doesn't say I'm some kind of a super therapist, it only indicates how fragile secret dating is compared to singles dating. When the secret daters discover there is no real bond between them, one of them may just need a little help to stop the secret dating.

When a mistress has an appointment, she frequently tells me within the hour that she is going to walk away from the affair. She expected, and even wanted, the affair to end. She just needed another person's confirmation that it would not work. Likewise, I have had appointments with male lovers who desired the same results.

Illicit love affairs are fragile

There are many reasons why an illicit love affair is much more fragile than a husband and wife relationship.

Any one of the following reasons is enough for secret dating to fail and for the marriage to persist:

1. If there are children that both parents love.

2. If there is no extra money.

3. If they do not want to share or separate their estate.

4. If there is an attachment to a house.

5. If there are relatives and friends that one will have to lose.

6. If there are moral obligations.

7. If there are church associations or other organizations that the couple have joined together.

8. If for a wife there is no way of supporting herself or her children with no occupation.

9. If there is a fear that the new relationship might not work.

Many times a marriage will persist, even those that should end in divorce for any one or more of the above reasons.

When does the secret lover fail?

Here is an extreme example of marital strength existing in a bad marriage:

I encouraged a couple who had a violent, abusive marriage to divorce, but they stayed together in spite of my urging. If there are reasons for the marriage to persist, it will persist. After a few experiences of trying to help these types of marriage end, I have ceased to encourage a divorce. If they want it to end, it will. Otherwise, they will tolerate a miserable union until death. If I can't end this type of marriage for a client, certainly a secret lover will not succeed. Secret love affairs in these cases almost always fail.

One of the major differences between the single dater and the secret married dater is that secret dating is frequently an attempt to find out if there is a better marriage possibility without paying a big price — divorce.

Another difference is that, at the time of the marriage, one of the spouses may not have been fully committed to the other which may cause that spouse to feel trapped. This non-committed spouse tries secret dating to find out if he has made the right commitment.

How Successful Is Secret Dating?

Can secret dating be successful?

Some affairs can be successful to a degree, even though they may last only for a few dates. The dating spouse may discover through the dating process that their husband or wife is not that undesirable and go home a more contented spouse.

Sometimes, when an affair is discovered, a dating husband moves out (either by request or on his own) but doesn't file a divorce action. He drops his dating friend and sets out to date a number of women. After a few month, he returns home a contented man. He remains faithful the rest of his married life.

Some spouses secretly date because of marital fatigue. The spouse is tired of the house, the kids, their partner, or a lack of personal attention. After a few dates this fatigued spouse discovers that the family is not so bad after all and returns home rejuvenated.

Secret dating could teach the spouse new leisure time activities or a different way of living or looking at things, due to discussions with the secret partner.

The above affairs were successful because the dating spouse discovered that his or her marriage was not so bad after all.

Alternatives to secret dating

On the other hand, if a dating spouse discovers that his or her marriage is terrible, then the secret dating could be considered successful only in the regard that it confirms the dating spouse's suspicions.

A secret dating spouse has several alternatives to end a secret relationship, whether successful or not:

1. He can disappear from the community. There may or may not be a divorce.

2. He can get a divorce and/or not marry for years.

3. He can get a divorce, not marry the lover, but eventually marry another.

4. He can marry the lover and remain permanently contented, or he can get a divorce after a year or so.

5. When he is discovered, the spouse can file an action, disappears with the children and the bank accounts. The dating spouse then mourns the loss of the children.

6. The spouse can move to another state, making it impossible for the dating spouse to visit the children.

7. Depending on the state in which a couple resides, the wife can get a divorce from the dating husband. She is then granted by the Court: the home, excellent alimony and child support. Frequently, she turns the children against the dating father.

8. The rejected spouse can see a therapist and then make an excellent second marriage if the complaints of the dating spouse are resolved by the

therapist.

9. The rejected spouse, if a husband, can get the children. This does happen in California. He marries a great new spouse and lives happily ever after. His ex-wife remarries within six months and the alimony ends.

10. The dating spouse can get the children, can make a bad marriage, then lose the children to the former spouse and lose out financially. Disasters just keep happening.

11. The dating spouse doesn't get a divorce because the lover dumps him. This spouse then lives a miserable married existence the rest of his life.

As you can see, unwed couples don't have these complications. They either marry or separate.

What can happen to the unwed lover?

She may be inexperienced, shy, a woman who had never engaged in sexual activities or has never gone anywhere. After a few months, she learns some new leisure time activities. She learns to cook. She learns to be good at sexual intercourse. She learns to dress the part. She is now an experienced 'married woman' although single.

She may marry the man she is seeing. They may have a great marriage, or it may end in divorce. She may decide to remain single and continue the dating game. She may dump him and go on to a successful marriage. She may decide to marry someone else and have an unsuccessful marriage. The affair could then remain the greatest experience of her life.

The single male may have similar experiences. He may have needed an experienced married woman to teach him how to live a married life. Having learned this, he dissolves the affair. He may then successfully marry.

From a moral point of view, an affair is not good. Affairs can also be disastrous, resulting in suicide or murder. But affairs have saved many marriages. Affairs can teach single persons how to prepare for marriage.

What everyone should know to survive love and marriage (whether an affair ends in marriage, divorce, or just ends) is that the participants do need psychotherapy. The fear, the helplessness, the neurotic behavior, the lack of personal skills and the need for secrecy are all indicators that a person needs to examine himself to make necessary personal changes to achieve happiness and success.

CHAPTER 13

CAUGHT IN AN AFFAIR

Amazing how many spouses having an affair get caught. A wife leaves the house in the morning, gets into the car and drives to the grocery store. On the way, she looks into the astray, notices that the lipstick color on the cigarette is different than hers. Her curiosity aroused, she sees that the brand name on the cigarette is different, also. He is trapped.

A husband gets up at 1:30 a.m. to get a drink of water. He sees his wife in the kitchen talking to someone on the phone. He thinks this is unusual. So instead of getting a drink, he decides to listen. As he listens, he is stunned. She is love talking to a male.

There is the anonymous phone call, telling a spouse that his or her spouse is having an affair and with whom. Lots of interesting information is revealed by the unidentified caller.

A husband never touches his wife's purse. Feeling safe, she leaves a love letter in it. This day he can't find his car keys. He goes to her purse to get her keys. Feeling around inside the purse he feels an envelope, pulls it out. The male name on the envelope is not a person he knows. He wonders why the man is writing his wife. He pulls the letter out of the envelope, unfolds it and the salutation reads, "Dear Sweetheart, I am missing you." He reads on. He cannot believe it. His wife is having an affair.

CHAPTER 13

Sometimes the mistress becomes exhausted when her lover puts off a divorce action, so she takes matters into her own hands and confronts the wife. He is exposed.

Sometimes a husband has a phone number in his wallet. The wife sees it. She has a friend call the number. A female answers. The friend asks to talk to the cheating husband by his first name. The female says, "He's not here just now." The wife knows now that her husband has a mistress.

There is perfume on his shirt that is not hers. There is lipstick on his collar. His wife suspects her husband is having an affair.

His wallet falls on the floor of his mistress' car. Her husband finds it. She is confronted and admits her affair.

The usual explanation offered for getting caught is that 'they wanted to get caught' — this is not usually true. In the excitement of lovemaking they forget some detail that gets them caught. It is difficult to always be that careful after so many dates. Inexperience on the first date can also trap a lover.

After the illicit couple makes a commitment to each other in the lovemaking relationship, they don't care if they get caught. They become bold. This is when they are apt to be detected.

There are those who never get caught. Why? They may be more alert or more cautious. They may care more about their children and his future with his wife. They may also have no intention of divorcing, or he may be experi-

114

enced at having affairs. Perhaps their spouses simply may not be that suspecting. There are many answers as to why some are not discovered.

Those who confess

Then there are those who probably will not be detected but nonetheless make a confession. Some are so disturbed by what they have done that they must make a confession, seeking forgiveness and reconciliation. They confess without thought as to what this might do to the married relationship or the other spouse as they attempt to clean their blackboard.

Some confess not for conscience reasons, but they just don't know how to dissolve the dating relationship or the marriage. They are too weak to move and so depend upon the other spouse to manage a solution. Whether the erring spouse wants a divorce or not, he waits helplessly for the other spouse to make a decision after his confession.

Some confess as a way of hurting the other spouse. Then having done this, they do everything they can to damage or destroy the other spouse and turn the children against them.

As a therapist, I am generally against confessing an affair to a spouse. I have found them to be more damaging than helpful. Confessions have resulted in divorce. They have damaged children. They have injured persons who in no way were involved. I am definitely in favor of secrecy. Marriages can terminate without the affair ever being revealed.

What happens when discovered?

There are the spouses who, for a variety of reasons, never reveal to their cheating partners the discovery of an affair. See the irony in the following situations:

The wife has ceased enjoying sexual intercourse with her husband. She is delighted that another woman is taking care of her husband's physical pleasure and has relieved her of this duty. She lets the affair continue. She is secure in the knowledge that a divorce will never occur.

In another situation, the innocent spouse is delighted. As the wife, she may have wanted the marriage to end, but for religious reasons could not file for a divorce having made a commitment. But now she feels justified in ending the relationship. She may never reveal that she knows about the affair, but will quietly go about making preparations for the termination of the marriage. Then comes the big surprise for the erring spouse when the attorney serves him with divorce papers. The dating spouse is shocked — particularly, if he was just playing around.

In still another situation, a frustrated spouse wants to have an affair but will not do so as long as the other spouse remains faithful, so plays the waiting game. Finally, the other spouse is found with a secret lover which frees the frustrated spouse to seek an affair. The erring spouse may never know this. Many times infidelity breeds infidelity. The marriage continues for whatever reason.

What may happen when an innocent spouse, who has always wanted out of the marriage, discovers that her husband is having an affair? She may ask her father, brother or friend to help expose her husband's infidelity to family and friends. Meanwhile, when the news trickles back to her, she pretends to be shocked about his infidelity. She then makes accusations, blaming the erring spouse. She may let others know about the affair, too. She may leave a note asking him to be gone by morning. Sometimes the erring husband just moves out. The wife returns home to find her husband's clothes gone and a note telling her that his attorney will be in touch.

If a husband is the innocent spouse, his reactions may be similar to the innocent wife's reactions. All the while the innocent spouse is secretly glad the affair happened. The innocent spouse escapes blame. He gets sympathy and, if Catholic, gets the priest's support.

What happens to the erring spouse?

The innocent spouse will react in a variety of ways. There is no standard way to react to the discovery of an affair.

I remember receiving a call from a couple in Hollywood. He was a producer and she an actress. They asked me to come to their home on a Saturday night. I rarely made house calls, but this time I made an exception.

They had a balcony which overlooked a beautiful, large living room. I sat in the living room listening to their reactions to the exposure of an affair. First, he would walk up the stairs, face me from the balcony and deliver his side of the triangle. Then she would walk part way up the stairs, face me and reply with her side. For an hour this drama unfolded before me, each taking turns on the balcony and stairway. Finally, I got them to sit down and talk. After they aired out all their complaints and unhappy issues with each other, their anxieties and hurt feelings subsided as they began to understand why they drifted apart from each other and why her husband sought comfort in an affair. That night after I left, they went to bed and had sex. This they revealed to me later. There was no divorce.

Another client, to woo his guilty wife back, burned their furniture and took the doors and windows out of the house. This was to let her know what could happen to her if she had any idea of leaving him.

One wife, finding her husband in an affair, invited a man into her home. She deliberately had sexual intercourse with him in her bed and let her husband discover them. This was one shocked man.

Still another wife, with a school teacher husband, discovered his mistress. She spooked him in a variety of ways in an attempt to end the affair. She would hide his car at night to prevent him from seeing his mistress. She would remove the spark plugs from his car so that he couldn't go to see her. When all else failed, she would drive to the mistress' house and honk the car horn. She won. They lived happily ever after.

Some husbands have held a loaded pistol to a wife's head and exacted a promise to end the affair. Some have beaten their wives.

Mistresses have been exposed at public meetings, fired from jobs, bought off by wives, raped and have had their cars bashed in, their tires slashed, etc.

Some wives have held on to their husbands and the man has not been able to escape. The mistress is thoroughly defeated and retreats from the scene.

Some wives commit suicide. The husbands then have to live with this on their conscience. They also face the accusations of their children for the rest of their lives.

Sometimes the outraged spouses join forces to make their guilty spouses cease an affair.

Sometimes married spouses, to end an affair, have had to take a job in another state or quit their job and seek employment in another city to avoid contact with a lover. Single individuals, too, have done the same.

Secret affairs — an attempt to maintain a marriage

Secret affairs are often an attempt to maintain a marriage. This is so frequently overlooked by the injured husband or wife, relatives and friends. The guilty spouse who is breaking an oath of fidelity is still trying to keep that oath, even while breaking it. This contradiction is difficult to comprehend for a spouse who discovers the affair. It is also difficult for the other illicit lover to grasp, although the lover may also have been trying to maintain a marriage.

If the innocent spouse wants their marriage to continue, he or she should know that secrecy is a means whereby the marriage has been maintained by the dating spouse. An affair can be a signal that the dating spouse does want to continue the marriage. What is probably needed to continue the marriage is psychotherapy.

The spouse, who is attempting to have an affair, should recognize that this temptation is a reason to seek psychotherapy and to solve the difficulty that way. Until millions of married individuals are convinced that psychotherapy is the way to resolve marriage frustrations and anxieties, there will be an increase in affairs.

Respect and trust needs to be reestablished for the couple's marriage to continue and many times, only a therapist can help restore a broken relationship.

Chapter 14

THERAPIST NEEDED

Dating couples may break-up naturally or because of external pressures. Either way, it is usually painful — certainly for the rejected one. Love affairs that are mainly for sexual pleasure break-up naturally, as these lovers are generally not the committed types. However, when a spouse is trying to find out something about his or her marriage relationship, there is no serious affectionate involvement. If the spouse picks a lover who is promiscuous, there is no emotional damage and the break-up is natural. If the spouse picks a serious individual, the break-up may be emotionally painful for both.

Low self-esteemed lovers

When one or both of the lovers have low self-esteem, it is difficult to escape from this type of love relationship. These lovers have probably not been successful at dating. They, having few leisure time activities, may immediately enter into a sexual relationship not knowing any other way to keep the relationship alive. If either of the lovers' knowledge and conversational skills are limited, this may prevent them from sustaining these relationships for any length of time.

If the relationship persists, it is probably because of a lot of sexual activity. This may be the only chance the lover will have to mate with another for one reason or another. After such an investment in affection, time commitment and perhaps money, the lover cannot afford to lose this love relationship. Many such affairs need the help of a therapist. One or both need psychotherapy. They also need psychotherapy to prevent future unhappy affairs. This will be a difficult relationship to end.

The neurotic personality

In some cases, one or both of the lovers may have a neurotic personality. One of the lovers may have temper tantrums and be verbally abusive while the other, having been humiliated during childhood and teen years, accepts the abuse. This relationship can result in marriage. This is called neurotic interdigitation. Many marriages are based on this condition.

Various individuals will date a neurotic personality. After some dating experiences, they will end the relationship as few can accept the severe anxiety attacks or other neurotic symptoms of the neurotic. The neurotic lover can be so critical and accusing that the other lover can accept it for only a limited time. The neurotic lover may also be helplessly dependent, and can only be accepted for only a limited time. These affairs break-up naturally if the lover is somewhat normal. However, if the lover is immature or also neurotic, then external help is needed.

Many neurotic or immature individuals may have enough good qualities that the dating lover who gets involved can't free himself from the entangling web. The begging, the self-pity, the bribery, the sexual intercourse, the physical attractiveness, the accusations, the blaming and the alibis of the neurotic entangles the lover and it seems impossible to break the tie. Only external help of a spouse, friend, psychologist, or even a move to another state will free him or her from the neurotic lover.

THERAPIST NEEDED

Sometimes two neurotic personalities get locked into an illicit affair and the only one who can free them is a therapist. Sometimes the innocent spouse needs the aid of an attorney and a therapist to resolve the situation.

The severely depressed

If a lover is a severely depressed individual, trying to end the affair is not only difficult, but it can be dangerous as the depressed lover may commit suicide. The non-depressed lover is unaware that the depressed lover has gotten into a serious emotional difficulty. This calls for the aid of a psychotherapist. Help from the outside is needed to end the relationship.

Sometimes a sense of responsibility on the part of a non-depressed lover forces him or her to continue a miserable relationship. Some marry the depressed lover not knowing what else to do or that professional assistance is necessary.

When a love affair ends for the severely depressed lover, he may have a depression that lasts from six months to a couple of years. He may substitute an institution, a pet for the lost lover or possibly join the military. Some women become nuns because they have been rejected.

These affairs need the help of a therapist. One or both need psychotherapy. They also need psychotherapy to prevent future unhappy affairs.

The alcoholic or drug abuser

There are love affairs which are based upon alcohol or drug abuse. The lovers cannot break the connection because they are too addicted. The innocent spouse may tolerate the affair, knowing that love is not involved. Alcoholic affairs frequently end in divorce for one of the lovers. The drinking or drug addicted couple may never marry but live together for awhile. Two drunks sometimes have enough sense not to marry.

Breaking up a love affair when one of the partners is either drug addicted or alcoholic is usually not easy. The therapist may not be able to solve the excessive drinking or drug addiction problems. Many times nothing less than a jail sentence, prolonged hospitalization or AA will work. The solution for a spouse when such an affair happens is divorce.

Many couples (whether married, single, or involved in illicit affairs) who want to avoid psychotherapy think that a better solution to breaking up is to become involved in another love relationship. This solution can work, but it doesn't solve other serious psychological symptoms. Sometimes, however, the lover who wants to escape remains attached to the old lover as well as the new lover. Now, he or she is worse off.

When everyone knows just how important it is to know the person you get involved with, then you will have a better chance for a successful marriage.

CHAPTER 15

WHAT KEEPS COUPLES LOYAL?

Millions of married couples in the United States do not have illicit affairs or seek a divorce. Many of these couples are just happy being married to their spouses. Their self-esteem is high. They plan events around their families. They respect the marriage vows, their spouses, family and friends.

Loyalty and commitment

Couples who have a deep sense of loyalty, not just in matters of love, are also loyal to parents, friends, schools and organizations. So it is natural for them to continue these loyalties after marriage. These couples appreciate each others:

They are courteous to each other.

They never feel that anyone owes them anything.

Each day they are glad that they found each other.

They enjoy taking care of each other.

They delight in surprising each other by doing something special.

They take care of themselves.

They don't impose upon each other.

When they disagree, it is not a contest to be won.

Each can correct mistakes in personal relationships with love.

A corrected mistake brings them closer together.

They have fun together.

They are not workaholics.

They enjoy their children.

They parent together.

They practice good self-management.

They communicate with each other freely.

They hold hands each day.

At night, they renew their union through hugging, kissing, words of appreciation, sharing happy memories and sexual relations. Through sexual union they become ever closer.

The peak moment in a couples' life is the wedding ceremony. The happy couple enjoys family living. Loyalty, respect and commitment to each other keep them together. The family unit for them is of utmost in their lives. Their religious beliefs also help to provide a secure environment for their marriage. Who could ask for anything more?

Unity of state and church

Many centuries ago, the marriage vows were effective under the Greek and Roman Catholic churches. Divorce in the Catholic Church was difficult for anyone to obtain, as King Henry VIII discovered.

The union of the state and church is illustrated in the story of *The Scarlet Letter* when the Puritan Church and the Colony of Massachusetts were one. Then the state enforced the church's commandments against illicit love affairs helping families to stay loyal to one another. The churches made the wedding vows a lifetime commitment. Divorce was relatively unheard of in those days.

A wall of separation

In 1787, the signing of the Constitution was purely a secular document defining only the powers of government. The Bill of Rights was quickly amended to the Constitution to protect the citizens' rights. The Bill of Rights is also secular, as Thomas Jefferson wrote to a friend, "... the purpose of the first amendment places a 'wall of separation' between Church and State in order to protect the individual's rights of conscience." These rights were backed by the states and social customs until World War II. Since then, the vows have been increasingly ineffective.

The effects of liberalizing the divorce law

The state governments, by liberalizing divorce laws have steadily withdrawn their support of the marriage vows. The steadily increasing ineffectiveness of the vows has contributed not only to increasing illicit love affairs and divorces, but also to a fear of married love. The lack of support from state and governmental laws have made the wedding just a lovely ceremony to millions.

Most clergymen and the public may not be aware of how many couples today who repeat the vows are not sincere or committed, thinking that if this doesn't work out they will dissolve the relationship. Marriage may also be thought of as a temporary arrangement, due to birth control and the lenient divorce laws. Parents, adults, brides and grooms feel justified in thinking this way because of the high divorce statistics of marriage today.

The family system in the United States has broken down over the years. The divorce rate is so high and complicated with second and third marriages, that the Department of Statistics can no longer provide a single figure. The effectiveness of the wedding vows now depends more upon the values of the couple.

Know the divorce laws

The modern couple lives in a complex society. While the fundamentals of family living has not changed, the modern couple cannot be ignorant about laws governing marriage and divorce. Couples need to be prepared and educated by taking classes in having a successful marriage and in picking out a suitable spouse.

Today couples can easily get a divorce. Where one spouse is guilty of an illicit love affair and the other loyal to the marriage vows, a divorce can easily be obtained by claiming irreconcilable differences. If there is cruelty, instability, drug or alcohol addiction by one spouse, a divorce will be granted when claiming irreconcilable differences as the reason for the divorce.

Attorneys are no longer under pressure to preserve a marriage as they have traditionally been in the past. Attorneys who specialize in family law will refer clients to psychologists, psychiatrist, clergymen and marriage counselors. These professionals will attempt to help clients resolve their difficulties through psychotherapy.

What Keeps Couples Loyal?

The effects of illegal sexual activities

Whatever happened to well over half of the married population who have participated in illicit love affairs, got divorced and indulged in promiscuous behavior? This is something that adults cannot ignore. Everyday parents, married couples, children and teenagers are suffering the consequences of it — rape, child molestation, intimidation, adulteries, abortions, and on and on. What ever happened to morality?

There are millions of dollars being spent on pornography. Millions are reading and viewing it. As far as I know, neither the psychology, the literature, nor the sociology departments are studying pornography or offering classes on the effects it has on marriage, or on the individual.

The miracle workers

When a marriage is in trouble, the couple needs to know that they can seek help from a religious institution, a psychologist, or a marriage counselor.

The professionals (psychologists, psychiatrists, and marriage counselors) are becoming more skilled, each year, in their field. They have made remarkable strides due to the advancing knowledge of science and technology. All of these professionals will become even more effective in helping couples solve their marital difficulties, whether seeking a divorce or solving many undesirable issues.

The drug and alcoholic addicts, the unstable, the psychotic, and severely depressed individuals will also be helped by the professional therapists and counselors in the family field. They will have had many years of resolving the social ills that plague our society today.

The pharmaceutical houses now have a drug that discourages alcoholics from craving alcohol to a large degree (the degree differs for each addict). This drug also doesn't make the alcoholic sick. It can help victims addicted cut back on drinking and speed up the recovery process. It can be prescribed by their general practitioner or therapist. This is a step in the right direction and maybe in the near future scientists will find a cure.

Yes! What the professionals will be able to do in the future will be unbelievable.

They will help thousands of couples find a happier married life.

They will help a high percentage of alcoholics and drug addicts.

They will help children with learning disabilities.

They will successfully help delinquent teenagers.

They will help to create a happier environment in the business community by working with business leaders.

When the ill effects of wars have passed and technology reaches its limit, the divorce rate will diminish and the family unit will enjoy happy relations with one another. Without loyalty, commitments and respect, no group will survive.

CHAPTER 16

VENEREAL DISEASE & ADDICTION

In the past, wars and military personnel caused venereal disease to spread, not so today.

An epidemic

Since 1975 venereal diseases (VD) have become epidemic. During the past ten years there has been an increase in new venereal disease types: genital herpes, chlamydia, AIDS, and more.

Papilloma virus of the genitals can cause cervical cancer in women. At the moment, new types of venereal diseases, not yet curable, are appearing. It behooves those with multiple sexual partners to watch out for diseases of sexual intercourse.

Condoms

Condoms still seem to be the best form of protection, as the military men of World War II discovered.

Military leaders tried to prevent the spread of venereal diseases by issuing condoms but met with opposition from the Vatican. The Catholic Church was caught in a bind. The popes were not against venereal disease control, but against birth control. Military leaders tried to control VD by the use of penicillin and other drugs.

I have known airmen in Japan to get syphilis several times. Plenty of wives and girl friends overseas and stateside have been infected by military men. US military men infected tens of thousands of women in many nations.

Venereal diseases

Some males and females are not at all cautious about venereal disease control. Women, who date and/or have affairs, use the pill or the diaphragm to prevent pregnancy. If they forget to protect themselves and become pregnant, an abortion ends the pregnancy. The easy availability of abortion and the quick cure for VD, until recently, caused many men and women to quit using rubbers on dates. Single women, or dating wives, by not insisting that men use condoms, have contributed to the spread of VD.

Many parents have contributed to the increase of VD by permitting teenagers:

1. to date freely;
2. to use drugs and alcohol;
3. to abandon chaperoning;
4. to use the car freely;
5. to use the pill or diaphragm with no warning that they can get VD by using these types of contraceptives.

The breakdown in personal self-management

The general breakdown in personal self-management has increased the spread of venereal disease. Now that herpes, chlamydia, and AIDS have made their appearance, sexual intercourse without condoms is risky, as there is no cure for some venereal diseases at this time. For those who are promiscuous, the risks are truly high.

Venereal Disease & Addiction

Before condoms appeared on the market, the fear of pregnancy and VD certainly kept millions of individuals from entering into an affair. Now with the condom, the fear of pregnancy has been reduced. Unfortunately, there is still an increase in affairs and VD due to the lack of self-management.

Many divorced individuals enter into sexual intercourse on the first, second, or third date without condoms. These individuals have contributed to the spread of venereal disease. Many of them engage in sexual activities before they know anything about a lover's character or his or her relationship with other individuals.

This is also true of the teenage set, particularly the thirteen to fifteen year olds, an age group who use the least caution. At least thirty percent of this group is having intercourse frequently. Parents of the junior high set today can't believe that this age group is taking drugs, using alcohol, and engaging in sexual activities.

Before World War II, parents of the junior high set would not permit any of these things to happen. Parents of this same age group in other nations have kept their teenagers under tight control. Since parents prior to World War II and parents of other nations controlled their junior high students, it would seem to me that the parents of today need to teach their children self-control.

Mothers feel safe about their daughters not getting pregnant by giving them birth control pills or a diaphragm, completely forgetting the possibility of VD.

Every endeavor of the scientific community to control birth seems to threaten the sexual fidelity as well as the health of individuals.

Our nation has been bombarded for the last few decades with drugs from across the border, making drugs easy to obtain and causing a drug epidemic across the United States. Many teenagers and adults have been caught in the web of addiction who were just trying to have a fun time and trying to keep up with their peers. Due to the illegal use of alcohol and drugs, teenagers and young adults have died by alcohol poisioning, by suicide and overdosing on drugs, mounting into the millions. This loss of life and health really may not justify the lives of patients who have been saved by drugs.

Unless a person learns to be sexually loyal and has a high degree of self-control, modern birth control can be a curse. Millions of sexually loyal couples are free from venereal disease. The cure of venereal disease and addiction to drugs is not condoms or penicillin shots, but an increase in sexual loyalty and sexual control.

Part IV - The Future Of Love & Marriage

CHAPTER 17

FAMILY & SEXUAL ETHICS

The best way to protect oneself from embarrassment, wrong choice of mate, unwanted pregnancy, loss of property and money is to practice family and sexual ethics. It is definitely a way to guarantee sexual enjoyment and no divorce.

Unfortunately, there is no system of family and sexual ethics that can completely guide one today in dating and marriage because of the radical changes in heterosexual relationships for the last seventy years. Except for a few professors, still few are trained adequately in this field.

What family members practice today is a makeshift of sexual ethics, part Christian and part whatever. These haphazard systems have failed to provide sexual enjoyment and successful family relationships for the couple. The clergy is often silent on this issue, failing to teach an adequate system of ethics for family members to follow.

The Catholic Church has a family and sexual ethical system, but parts of the system need to be updated.

The family and sexual ethical systems of the Protestant denominations have little instructions in the ethics of dating and in the ethics of marriage relationships. The clergymen have almost quit teaching whatever is left of each denominations' ethical systems.

For many couples, what little ethical system they may have acquired begins to fail the day of the marriage ceremony. Why?

Since most engaged couples are not tested or go through any type of screening process to determine whether they are prepared for marriage — morally and/or psychologically — to take the wedding vows for better or for worse.

Few clergymen prepare a bride and groom to determine whether they are or will be competent spouses and parents, or whether they are alcoholic, drug addicted, or in need of psychotherapy.

Some psychologist, however, do test to find out if a couple is suited for one another. One such popular personality test, Meyer & Briggs, is still being used successfully on couples to discover more about who they are to marry.

A few brides and grooms may need professional help before the wedding ceremony; more need psychotherapy within the year.

Couples need to know that

1. Being in love doesn't guarantee that a marriage will never need repair;

2. They are not automatically competent to be spouses and parents;

3. They need to be tested to determine whether they are or will be competent spouses and parents.

A psychologist or clergymen should at least warn the couple if one of them needs to change if the marriage is to succeed.

A preacher performing the wedding ceremony may say to the bride and groom as he hands each their ring, "This is a symbol of your eternal love." This is preacher's language. With today's high divorce rate, it is an inappropriate statement. The average length of a marriage today for at least over fifty percent may be less than ten years.

The preacher, the priest or the rabbi should say, **"The ring is a pledge of sexual loyalty."** This pledge is the foundation of family and sexual ethics. At the time of the wedding ceremony this ethical statement of sexual loyalty is important because many marriages are ending by the route of illicit love affairs.

The least the ring should mean ethically to other men and women who see it — **"This is my man or woman, please don't tempt. We will remain sexually loyal to each other."**

A spouse, who may want to engage in an illicit affair, may encourage another person to kiss and hold hands. They may justify an affair to themselves and others by saying, **"The marriage was breaking up any way. Therefore, I am not responsible for making an unethical decision."**

It may be true that the marriage was ending, but the ethical answer for the lover to say would be, **"I could be in love with you. If you think you can love me, then go home and tell your spouse the marriage is over and seek a divorce. If you are not sure, seek the aid of a psychologist or** a psychiatrist. I can wait for you to resolve your marital difficulties. Until you do this, I cannot date you."

This is an ethical answer that parents and clergymen should be training a teenager, a spouse, or a dating person to say to someone who is tempted to break a vow.

An engagement ring symbolizes a commitment on the part of both male and female. This ring is a signal to other males, **"Don't touch my woman. She is important to me."** Wearing the engagement ring still symbolizes this meaning for many teenagers and college students. This is another small part of sexual ethics.

The clergy performing the wedding vows should counsel the couple before the ceremony by saying: **"If you start faltering in your sexual loyalty, seek professional help to repair it. If it is not reparable, file for divorce. Don't involve yourself in an affair because you lack the courage to end the marriage."** One reason why clergymen don't say this to couples is that it suggests they approve of divorce.

Clergymen teach the traditional supports for Christians — Bible reading, prayer, attending service or mass on Sundays. These are wonderful supports, but many times they do not solve marital difficulties as over half of the married couples are divorced today. For many priests and preachers, to suggest psychotherapy as a solution seems to indicate a weakness of belief in the church's traditional supports.

In private practice, I have found that psychotherapy usually works better for Christians with severe difficulties than the traditional supports — church attendance, prayer and Bible reading.

I am not against the methods of the priests or the preachers. These supports are very important along with psychotherapy. I have helped Catholics, Jews and Christians become stronger in their faith.

Many couples get married without having the necessary information they need to make their marriage a success. Many couples have no idea how much knowledge it takes to be a successful partner and parent. There are no courses given to these young people today on either ethical behavior, on child training or on sexual loyalty.

The school system is now, however, teaching young adults courses in the human reproductive system and the importance of practicing safe sexual activity. But it should tag on lessons of sexual ethics and sexual loyalty.

In order to keep from destroying the family as we know it today, sexual ethics and sexual loyalty need to be an important subject for children growing up. These are the subjects that need to be taught in all the churches and schools everywhere. An incentive for teenagers and young adults could be included, such as pledging sexual abstinence, denoting loyalty with a silver ring until marriage when a golden ring binds two as husband and wife. A united family is what makes a nation strong and life worth living.

Parents should also be taking courses in sexual ethics to reinforce the clergyman's efforts in making the family a happy, successful institution.

In today's society many young couples are afraid of marriage and are living with one another, not trusting the sanctity of marriage.

Marriage has not become a safe secure stage in life for many young people as they have seen the fighting and battles going on with their fathers and mothers. The insecurity that many young folks have had to endure, reflects all their fears of today. They, by themselves, have figured out a way to escape the marriage break-ups, divorce, and all the nasty battling and hurt feelings that they have experienced.

But, to their amazement, many young folks are finding out that they can't escape the hurt feelings when a relationship breaks up, married or living together. They are discovering that whenever there is a breakup, it hurts — yes, both parties are hurt. Granted, they do not have the legal obligation of marriage or children to consider, but nonetheless the break-up affects both of them.

The women of today are working a full-work week, or half-work week and many can support themselves. Many women have their Bachelor of Science degrees, Master degrees, and sometimes a Ph.D. Some women are professionals— doctors, lawyers, judges, CEOs, etc. The women's liberation movement has not helped the family stay together.

What is needed to save the family unit?
There is a need for courses in sexual ethics for young people growing up, for married couples and for divorced couples. Sexual ethics are developing haphazardly — through trial and error.

Current dating ethics are:

1. That divorced women with children do not let men stay overnight in their homes. This is to establish in the minds of the children that only legalized sex is permitted.

2. That mother keeps control of her sexual life so that father cannot ask for custody of the children.

3. That divorced women keep the men they are dating away from their children, so the children don't have to be concerned with the prospect of each new male becoming their new father. When mother makes her decision as to whom her new husband will be, she can then invite him to the home.

Children really don't like the idea of a dating mother when they already have a father even though he is living in another place. They still hope that mother and dad will get back together, even after the divorce is final.

Everyone needs ethical guidelines

There is no formal standard yet. Especially in dating.

Is it proper for a mother to ask the date to pay for a babysitter because she can't afford it?

Does he quickly exchange resumes with her to save time and money if he is looking for a spouse?

Should he immediately tell her that he is just out for fun and a night in bed and probably no return dates?

141

If he is just out for fun and many dates, but no marriage intended, does she share expenses and vice versa?

Does the female think that she has to pay her way by having sexual intercourse? If so, is this considered prostitution?

I have raised some of the ethical questions for daters, brides and grooms, divorced and married. There are many more questions to be considered.

There is currently little or no formal guidance by professional leaders. Until new formal ethics are created for Christians, as well as non-Christians, there will be increasing confusion, emotional damage, unwanted pregnancies, ill-advised marriages and unnecessary divorces.

Everyone who dates, secret or otherwise, needs ethical guidelines.

CHAPTER 18

THE FUTURE OF LOVE & MARRIAGE

When the 21th century began, the heterosexual revolution was not complete. What will survive of the traditional relationships between men and women? The answer rests with the Protestant, Roman Catholic and Jewish lay people, not the preachers, pope, priests, or rabbi.

What are the freedoms that women have achieved since World War I?

1. Freedom to smoke, to drive a car, to use drugs, to use profanity.
2. Freedom to dress as they desire.
3. Freedom to have sexual information.
4. Freedom from sexual loyalty.
5. Freedom from male authority.
6. Freedom from total parenting.
7. Freedom from segregating men and women.
8. Freedom of occupational choice.
9. Freedom from pregnancy.
10. Freedom of movement.
11. Freedom to be sexually aggressive.
12. Freedom to be assertive.
13. Freedom of politics.
14. Freedom of education.

How will the use of these freedoms by women affect the heterosexual relationships of men and women in the future?

How will they affect husband and wife, parent and child and dating relationships?

Fifty years from now, after many of these radical changes in heterosexual relationships become custom, a new code of ethics will be worked out leading to more pleasant and beneficial relationships between men and women, parent and child.

Men and women will always date and marry. The foundation of married love is based on years of love or lack of love experiences that every boy and girl has had with his or her mother. I expect that in the future married men and women will really enjoy one another more than they do today.

Children will certainly enjoy their fathers more than in past generations, as men will have more leisure time.

Over half of the couples who marry will definitely enjoy a sustained marriage. Their children will be more successful in school and with playmates than children who come from divorced homes.

As the number of unwanted children diminish there should be greater numbers of happier individuals because their parents wanted them. This should mean they will be better functioning spouses, when it's their turn to marry.

Within the next fifty years, many couples will seek counseling to prevent a divorce. In the future, those who have doubts about their forthcoming marriages hopefully will seek counseling before marriage to ensure their marriages will succeed.

The major reason for the improvement in marital relationships in this century will be due to the availability of marriage counselors, psychologists, psychiatrists, clergymen, educators and child development experts.

With a growing number of therapists who are becoming more skillful, there should be an increasing number of happier spouses and fewer divorces.

At the present time, what is needed are courses in human relationships, in child care for girls and boys at grade school and high school levels. Courses are also needed for young adults in dating and marriage. Such courses will reduce all types of social ills. After fifteen years of teaching these courses to millions of students, the divorce rate should drop drastically and the quality of the family should improve markedly.

The physical fitness movement and women's participation in athletics and other types of physical recreation should also improve the quality of marriage and the health of spouses. Couples should enjoy each other more as they share these interests and skills.

As sexual knowledge increases and the number of frigid women (who cannot climax) diminishes, there should be fewer illicit affairs.

When men change their masturbation fantasies and are taught sexual courtesy, there will be less fearful relationships between men and women. This will lead to happier spousal relationships.

As the community demands lessen for men to marry, more men will chose to be single. As sex education becomes available, more men will lead a celibate life.

As women do not have to earn a living by marrying, they will remain single in larger numbers, too. There has always been that choice to remain single, as nuns and priests have known. Other men and women, through the centuries, have made that choice, too, although not for religious reasons.

When both men and women become aware of how much academic and guided training one needs to be a parent, more couples will elect to be childless. Those who do choose to be parents will seek training, thus rearing happier children. In turn, their children will marry and produce happy children too.

Those who marry in the future should be happier because they have more choices now than any time in history.

Hopefully, in the future, the workaholic business leader, who is now more concerned with production and increased sales volume, will be as concerned for the welfare of the families and children of his employees. Married love will then improve.

THE FUTURE OF LOVE & MARRIAGE

When business leaders are more concerned about the sexual activities of the business and political community, this, too, will improve dating and married love

If the work week is reduced to thirty hours, the enjoyment of working will improve. Men and women will have time to share parenting, participating in community activities as well as spending more time with relatives and friends.

The activities of the marketplace will then be geared not just to bottom line thinking, but protecting family activities and not destroying them.

The sexual roles of the male and female are changing. This should lead to better husband and wife relationships and to better sexual relations.

Many professionals of the future will be able to minimize the number of neurotic and psychotic behavioral symptoms as well as addictions and fears of all kinds. This will reduce the divorce rate greatly and cause better heterosexual relationships.

Until everyone becomes aware of the damaging effects of warfare to the individual and the family and develops ways to protect the family from its destructive effects, heterosexual relationships and family life will always deteriorate.

If there is no intercontinental war for fifty years or more, family life will improve remarkably.

CHAPTER 18

Hopefully, juvenile delinquency will be drastically reduced by another century. Love and marriage between men and women should become far more enjoyable. The love relationships of person to person should be better.

I believe an era of delightful human relationships is near.

This Is A Mature Adult

Francis H. Wise, Ph.D. 1973

A Person:

who can organize time
    Is an efficient adult;
who protects animals, human beings, plants, and
    property
    Is a humane and loving adult;
who can disagree pleasantly and effectively
    Is a peaceful adult;
who can give attention and who can listen
    Is a wise adult and a good conversationalist;
who can be considerate of another person
    Is a thoughtful and appreciative adult;
who knows how to achieve goals
    Is a successful adult;
who knows how to control his body
    Is a healthy adult;
who knows how to be self-entertaining
    Is never a lonely adult;
who knows and can live within his limitations
    Is not a frustrated adult;
who knows how to forgive
    Is a loved and loving individual;
who is not afraid to defend himself
    Will not be a humiliated adult;
who is not afraid to be hurt
    Will not be a fearful adult;
who is not afraid to die
    Is a serene adult;
who can worship
    Is an orderly adult;

A Person:

who can sacrifice
>Will be a leader of adults;

who can save
>Need not fear old age

who pays his bills on time;
>Is not a harassed adult;

who truly knows how to learn from his mistakes
>Is not an opinionated adult, but a child of God;

who understands the purpose of authority
>Is a cooperative adult;

who accepts routines, rules, and laws of a group —
>be it family, club, school, church, or state
>Is a harmonious adult;

who can control himself through routines, rules, and laws
>Is an independent adult;

who can accept standardized patterns of living
>Is a respected adult;

who can accept changes and difficulties in daily living
>Is a stable adult;

who can control his behavior upon the basis of generalizations
>Is an intelligent adult;

who can control his feelings
>Is a happy adult;

who can enjoy living
>Has mastered these skills and is

A Mature Adult

INDEX

INDEX

INDEX

INDEX

154

INDEX

INDEX

INDEX

www.ingramcontent.com/pod-product-compliance
Lightning Source LLC
Chambersburg PA
CBHW052007090426
42741CB00008B/1582